Counsel from Psalm 119

Jay E. Adams

TIMELESS TEXTS
Woodruff, SC

Commentary Text and
Translation of Psalm 119
Copyright © 1998
Jay E. Adams

ISBN 1-889032-07-7

Printed in the United States of America.

INTRODUCTION

Psalm 119 has to do with the Scriptures. Every verse (with the possible exception of verse 122, which is probably due to a scribal transcription slip) speaks of the Bible under one of ten or eleven different terms. While each of these descriptive words in itself describes something fresh about the Bible that the others do not, they are so close in intent and meaning that, in this Psalm, the variation of terms is usually, if not wholly, a matter of style. We shall treat them synonymously except where it is obvious that the peculiar nuances of the word are of significance to the meaning and application of the verse.

While speaking of terms, it might be important to note that the word "Psalm" (*tehilim* in Hebrew and *Psalmoi* in the Greek Septuagint) means "praise." But it is not merely praise alone that is denoted; both the Hebrew and the Greek words, at root, have the idea of playing musical instruments. The words, then, mean "to sing praise to accompaniment."

Psalm 119 is divided into twenty-two sections, each containing eight verses. The twenty-two sections correspond to the twenty-two letters of the Hebrew alphabet. Each verse in the Hebrew, within each section, begins with the letter to which that section is devoted. This acrostic arrangement probably was designed for mnemonic purposes. A Jewish student learned his ABCs through memorizing these great truths about the Bible. While in translation the verses cannot be made to conform to the letters of the English alphabet, memorizing the Psalm is still a good goal for young Christians to set.

Of what particular value does Psalm 119 have to the counselor? Several might be noted here and more as we

Introduction

continue. First, individual verses, like those in Proverbs, doubtless, will be of value for counselors to expound, apply and then ask counselees to memorize so that they may use them as "Portable truth." (See the volume on Proverbs in *The Christian Counselor's Commentary* series for an explanation of that term.) Second, since every verse in one way or another points to the Scriptures, the importance of and the need for learning and living according to the Bible is brought forward by the Psalm (precisely what most Christians need to learn). Moreover, there is much particularized help for afflicted, suffering, sinning, puzzled Christians—just the stuff of which counseling is made. All-in-all, you will probably find Psalm 119 as helpful as any book in the Bible for use in counseling once you have come to know it and learn how to use it.

But now, for the Psalm itself.

Psalm 119:1

ALEPH

Aleph (above) is the first letter of the Hebrew alphabet. Throughout this book you will read such headings. Understand that these, appearing at the head of each section, are the names of the letters of the Hebrew alphabet.

**1 Happy are those who are complete in their way;
Who walk in Yahweh's law.**

The word **happy** or "blessed" indicates that the one so designated is walking *in all areas* of his life in the Lord's **way**. That is the only road to true happiness. Now if there is one thing for which counselees are continually searching, it is happiness. The Hebrew word *tam* (complete) is the equivalent of the Greek *teleios*, used in James 1 (see the commentary on James in the above-mentioned series for an exposition of the Scriptural idea of *completeness*). It does not imply sinless perfection, but, rather, a lifestyle (**way**) that is, in each area, growingly conforming to **Yahweh's Law**. There is no area of the person's life in which the Scriptures do not have some impact. The word *tam* is used in Job 1:1 as a description of Job.

It is not of small import that God makes it clear from the outset that the way to happiness is through conformity to the Bible. Counselees who refuse to do what the Bible teaches *cannot* be **happy**. Of course they may find momentary happiness in things, happenings, people, etc., but there is no bedrock, lasting joy that underlies their lives—especially in time of heartache and trial. It is that sort of happiness-joy of which the verse speaks. This verse and the next two form a sort of introduction to the

1

Psalm 119:2

whole of the Psalm, just as Psalm 1, which also emphasizes the same thing, stands as an introduction to the entire book of Psalms.

> **2 Happy are those who keep His testimonies;
> Who seek Him with the whole heart.**

The **testimonies** of God are, of course, His Scriptures. The word **testimony** occurs 23 times in Psalm 119 and indicates *those things to which God witnesses.* The word **Law**, occurring 25 times, means *that which points the way.* The Scriptures point the way to go (are a guide to the Christian traveling through life) by mandating his actions in various situations of life.

But notice how the verse puts the finger on the common problem that many counselees have: it says the happy Christian is the one who follows Yahweh's **testimonies with his whole heart**. There is no place for divided loyalties, halfheartedness. Too many counselees want to pick and choose those testimonies that they wish to follow and reject those that they have no intention of following. That cannot be. Counselors, while stressing that they do not expect perfection in this life, must at the same time opt for a wholehearted desire and effort to grow in every area of life, so that the counselee truly can be said to be *tam*. While working on one thing at a time (he can't do everything at once), a counselor must not let the counselee think that he may serve God only in certain aspects of his life. There is a danger in that. As you work with him in one area, it might be well to keep on saying such things as, "I am anxious for you to get this in hand so that we can move on to the rest of those things that God requires." Keep making the point.

The only alternative to perverse living is biblical living. The world doesn't know that and is always trying to convince your counselees that it is not true. Counselees will therefore suggest other ideas, opposed to the **testimonies** of God in the Bible, ideas that they have learned elsewhere. Make it plain that if they wish to please God, the course of life that they must learn to pursue can be found in the Bible alone.

Notice that the place to **seek** God is in the Bible. Counselees will find Him and His will for their lives nowhere else. Mystics think that they can have encounters with God apart from the Scriptures. They think that nothing need come between them and God (not even Christ, nor the Bible). They therefore work up some sort of "experience" they suppose to be the presence of God in this manner and look down on the "peons" who try to find God in the Scriptures. If you detect any element of this in a counselee, work hard to expunge it from the beginning. It is dangerous (semi-mystical ideas of those who seek guidance elsewhere are described in my book *The Christian's Guide to Guidance*).

3 They also do not practice perverseness;
They walk in His way.

The word translated **practice perverseness** has in it the idea of deceitful, tricky, insidious depravity. The thought in using this rather comprehensive term seems to be that all of these wicked ways may be avoided only by **walking** in God's **ways**. The import of the term **way** as a description of the Bible is that the place to find the right style of life to live is in the Scriptures. **Ways** are the paths, the roads that one **walks**. They are, therefore, the habitual responses that one develops from having pursued these paths. The **ways** that please God can be found only in the Bible. Thus, if a counselee wishes to change his **ways**, he must replace the practices of perversity with their biblical alternatives. That is what counseling involves. That is why counselors who want to help counselees must come to know and learn to use the Bible well.

4 You have commanded us to carefully keep your precepts.

The word **precepts**, occurring 21 times in the Psalm, means "mandates handed down to be observed." When God mandates something, He doesn't do so for His own benefit but for ours. We should listen to what He requires and do as He says. He expects His **precepts**, mandates, to *be observed*. But there is another word in the verse that is of importance, the word translated **carefully**. It means, literally, "very much." The **observance of God's commandments** is to be done well. One must give himself to the pursuit of holiness. It is not enough to put forth a half-hearted, feeble effort to **observe** them. God expects counselees to give themselves to the pursuit with energy and faithfulness: **carefulness**.

Part of that care is for the counselee to begin to become a Bible student. It is not enough to take what a counselor says on his word alone (too many so-called biblical counselors tell counselees many things that they cannot substantiate biblically). The counselee must be a good Berean who knows how to "search the Scriptures daily" to see whether what a counselor says is so (cf. Acts 17:11). Moreover, once a counselee is dismissed from counseling, if he has not been shown the importance of learning to use the Scriptures practically, but has depended solely on what the counselor has given him, he will likely continue to get into trouble since he is unable to glean truth from the Scriptures for himself. My suggestion is to give every person who "graduates" from counseling a copy of a book like *What to Do on Thursday,* which, if followed, will help him to become a practical student of Scripture. And, along with the book, make it clear that this will be the way to stay out of counseling and to stay in God's favor in the future. It is important not only to instill a love of the Scriptures in counselees, but to urge them to become students of the Bible, learning to study and apply the precepts of God with care.

**5 O that my ways were fixed
To keep Your statutes!**

Here is a prayer sigh we all utter from time to time! What counselor can help but utter it? A **statute** (the word is used 20 times in the Psalm) is "something that is engraved, cut." That is to say, it is a definitive standard, set forth in a manner that is intended to last (like a tombstone). The fixed nature of God's will is important; He doesn't change with the wind or the times. That is why we can trust what the Bible says. The Scriptures are etched in stone. They are dependable in every generation (cf. I Corinthians 10:6; Romans 15:4). If only our ways were as **fixed** ("settled, established") and firm as the Bible itself! That is the Psalmist's prayer—and should be ours. And it is the spirit that a counselor should communicate to every counselee. It is with that attitude that men and women become *tam*.

**6 Then I will not be ashamed
When I look to all Your commandments.**

This verse is a continuation of the previous one—a second stanza to the sigh! When one's ways are as **fixed** as the **commandments** of God (those things He requires, enjoins with authority; the word is used 22 times in Psalm 119), then he will have no reason to be embarrassed or ashamed of his behavior. Many counselees come into

Psalm 119:7

counseling humiliated, ashamed. That is because of behavior that is out of kilter with what God requires. Get them to see this and they too will sigh with the Psalmist.

Notice, one may be doing fairly well in many areas of his Christian life, but there may be one or two in which he isn't progressing as he should. The shame comes from that; he fails to keep **all** of God's **commandments**. People who are highly respected for what they do accomplish in the Christian world may not rest on their laurels. They should thank God for what He (not they) has achieved in their lives. But they may still be withholding something. They could very well be **looking** the other way when they should be looking at what God says! Check out **all** around the circle of their lives to see what the shame stems from. You will find something where shame prevails.

**7 I will thank You with integrity of heart
When I have learned Your righteous
    judgments.**

The word **judgments** is a legal term meaning "decisions handed down." These were court verdicts (case law) divinely given. Many counselees fail to honor God in their lives for lack of **learning**. The importance of learning the ways God has determined many specific things in life must be emphasized. To learn, however, is to learn *to observe*, not merely to learn to locate or to recite. When one has done as the Psalmist says, he will have good reason to **thank God**. After all, he will not have achieved this on his own. Make it plain to a counselee that every achievement is the result of the enlightenment and the power of the Spirit at work in his life. On the other hand, he may take full credit for every failure!

**8 I will keep Your statutes;
Don't forsake me entirely!**

Here is the determination of the true saint of God. He wants to observe God's **statutes** so as to please Him, but as he looks at the results of his endeavors, he wonders how the Lord can continue to put up with him. All he can figure is that God has every right to **forsake him** (give up on him) **entirely**. But God is a God of grace. Make that clear to discouraged counselees. He will not give up on us, even when we are ready to give up on ourselves! Don't let counselees who are not merely feigning or who are not really interested in making progress give up. Make it clear that if they cry out to God as the Psalmist does He will hear and He will help. Change comes hard—as many of the verses in this Psalm will indicate. But the idea throughout is that one must stick to it, no matter what.

BETH

**9 How shall a young man purify his way?
By guarding it according to Your word.**

Surely, if any passage of the Scriptures applies to youth this does! The **young man** in counseling is a problem. There is no doubt that the teenager is one of the most difficult counseling subjects you will face. Because many of them are still riding the crest of the wave, which has not yet broken, and they have not yet come crashing down on the coral beneath, they are hard to move. You, of course, cannot do it anyway—God must do so by His Spirit. The Spirit works through His Word. If a youth is caught in fornication, in drugs, in a rebellious lifestyle, there is only one solution to his problem: if he heeds

Psalm 119:10

God's Word, he can **purify** his lifestyle. Conversely, for him to avoid a way of life that will bring dishonor and ruin to him and to his family, he must **guard** his life according to those directions that he finds in the Bible. If there is anything, then, that you can do for a youth, it is to direct him to the Bible. Make him understand that every decision he makes he is making not over against you and what you have to say, or over against his parents and their advice, but over against God. That may be done only by clearly delineating what the Bible says. Using the twelfth chapter of Ecclesiastes and the book of Proverbs is one very helpful way to address youth.

When you are working with a young person who is caught up in "youthful lusts" never forget that sanctification is through the truth, and that God's Word is truth (John 17:17). The word, sometimes translated "keep," means **guard**. It is used, for instance, in Genesis 3:24. If Adam had guarded the garden as he should have (in Genesis 2:15 the same word is used) he would not have sinned. If a youth guards the way that he goes according to the Bible, he will avoid much sin. (Also, cf. II Timothy 2:19-22; I Timothy 5:2.)

10 With my whole heart I have searched for You;
Let me not wander from Your commandments.

How foolish for one who has wholeheartedly sought God in His Word, now to **wander** like a straying sheep from those things that he has learned. All that energy, time and effort wasted! The joy he experienced left behind! This is especially sad for those who have been faithful Bible students but have somehow fallen into some terrible mess. Remind them of the verse and what it teaches. The prayer is uttered out of great frustration. It is, therefore, one to turn to when you find a counselee who is frustrated and is about to give up. Point out that even the inspired writer sometimes likewise found himself frustrated but, instead of giving up, prayed like this and once again sought God in His Word. You can be sure God heard.

**11 I have stored Your Word in my heart,
So that I might not sin against You.**

This is the verse for every sinning counselee who, having been forgiven by God and man, now sets out afresh on his course. Remind him that if he has hidden God's Word in his heart as portable truth, that will keep him from sin in the future (see comments in the introduction about "portable truth").

It was because Jesus Christ had God's Word in His heart that He was able to withstand the temptation of the evil one in the desert. Each time He was able to quote an appropriate passage of Scripture in answer to the enemy's suggestion. When truth from the Bible is at the front of your mind at all times—fresh because you continually study, memorize and meditate on it—you will be able to guard your way as you ought. If a counselee does not have truth readily available **in his heart**, he will be confused about what actions to take. He will be susceptible to wrong suggestions, will not be able to evaluate what he hears and sees, and will be at the mercy of the world, the flesh and the devil. It is crucial, therefore, not only to base counseling on the Bible and to use the Bible in sessions, but also to encourage counselees to begin a systematic Bible study program that they assiduously follow at all times (cf. notes on v. 4).

Psalm 119:12

Everyone has something in his heart. He can't avoid it. Often, it is full of wrong things that must be replaced with the Word of God. Whatever is in his heart motivates your counselee (cf. Proverbs 4:23). That is important to remember. You might even test a counselee at some point in a session. In reference to some problem he faces—say, a temptation to speak nastily in return for nasty, abusive language of another directed to him—ask your counselee, "Can you quote a verse of Scripture that would help you to reply differently?" If he can't come up with Proverbs 15:1, Ephesians 4:29-31, Romans 12:14 or a comparable verse, you can refer to this verse in Psalm 119 and then point out to him the importance of storing verses in his heart so that they will guide him in times of temptation. Make it clear that one of the reasons he failed in the most recent attempts to change is precisely because he did not have the Bible in his heart where the Spirit could use it to impress its truth upon him.

**12 You are happy, Yahweh;
Teach me Your statutes.**

This prayer includes a confession of ignorance, the desire of the true Bible student, a doxological explicative and strong feeling. God is **happy**, One to be blessed because of Who He is and what He has done. It is He Who has provided the Bible for His children. What a wondrous gift! Here, in our very hands we may hold the Word of God! How marvelous are His mercies to us. Since He has been so gracious as to provide truth in this propositional fashion, surely we should, with the Psalmist, declare our desire to know more and more of it! Truly, we all know so little. Until you are able to ascertain a hunger for God's truth (not just a desire to get something, or to be rid of some burden) in a counselee, you may be relatively sure that he will be headed for more trouble in the future. It is this thankful desire to know more of the Bible and to be able to put it into practice in one's life that makes all the difference. Keep that in mind. If you focus only on the problem(s) he presents and fail to instill in him a love for God's Word, you have not really done *biblical* counseling. True nouthetic counseling is Bible-based, Bible-centered in every respect. It always focuses on the importance of the Bible for the counselee's present *and future* welfare.

**13 With my lips I have declared
All the judgments of Your mouth.**

It is important, as I have said, to hide God's word in your heart in order not to sin against Him. But that isn't the only reason for so storing up those truths. One must be able, at a moment's notice, to be able to speak to others about them. The heart should move the mouth. If it is not clear what the Psalmist here has in mind, think of this: here is a counselee who has been helped by learning, following and storing up God's truth within his heart. Now, should that be the end of it? Of course not! In order to spread the honor of God and the glory of His Word, he should also be willing to tell others what God has done for him. Moreover, he must be able at any time to help another who is in trouble by **declaring** the truths that he knows are applicable to his situation. No one should keep good news to himself. This is true of the gospel; but it is true also of all that God does for one after he is saved. Less counseling would be necessary if Christians were regularly repeating the Scriptures to one another in appropriate ways in appropriate circumstances. If a counselee truly appreciates what has happened to him by means of the Bible then he ought to tell others so. If you inherit a

Psalm 119:14

fortune, you surely will tell all those you love, won't you? How can you keep it in? It is important, however, to warn counselees not to brag about their change, but simply express heartfelt appreciation to God and to others for what He has done to effect it.

**14 I have rejoiced in the way of Your testimonies
As about all riches.**

Continuing the thought at the end of the previous verse, here the Psalmist says that he is as happy about the way that God's testimonies guide him as he would be about receiving an abundance of **riches**. That is the way you want your counselees to leave counseling—rejoicing about what God has done for them through His Word (not telling everyone what a wonderful counselor you are!). Help every counselee you can to view the Bible as a treasure chest full of riches that are his, and that are obtainable nowhere else. Surely, no Rogerian, Freudian, Adlerian or follower of Maslow could talk about the principles and practices of such men that way! You have something unique. Never forget that. And don't let the counselee forget it either. Having seen how the Bible meets his needs and problems, how it directs him in the way, you should help him to develop a new appreciation for it. Truly, it is nothing less than a treasure.

**15 I will meditate on Your commandments
And I will regard your ways.**

Biblical meditation is not a matter of peeling the onion, layer after layer as one looks within. It is not introspective. Notice, meditation is centered not on self but on God's Word. When one meditates, he is looking at the truth of a passage from all sorts of angles. It is like turning the diamond so as to be able to view the colors that flash from every facet. Meditation is a matter of relating life to Scripture. One must think of how a passage applies. That, and nothing less, is what the Psalmist is talking about. He **regards** the **ways** of God shown by the **commandments** of God with care and concern so as to understand, apply and be able to implement them. The idea of meditation, then, is not an inner thing. It is meditation on objective truth that leads to change in one's lifestyle. A counselee from time to time may be told this and then sent home to meditate on the Bible in relationship to his situation. As a result, he should have a page or two of notes from the meditation, along with a plan of action that grows out of it. The Scriptures, undigested, do little good. Teach rumination on the Bible.

**16 I will delight myself in Your statutes;
I will not forget Your Word.**

Perhaps enough has been said about the joy of learning and living Scripture. This verse reiterates all that I have written before. But it goes on to make a promise to God. Here is one that every Christian counselee should make. That is, that he **will not forget God's Word**. Not to do so is the crux of faithfully living the Christian life. It is a determination that each should make. But if he is undisciplined, he will slacken and soon **forget**. It is not easy to remember all that one has learned. That is why he needs the constant refreshment of daily study. While in counseling, if a counselee begins to study the Bible regularly, as you should encourage him to, he may be able to develop the discipline to continue after he leaves counseling. Check up on his study habits regularly (each session). At any rate, taking personal responsibility for the study of Scripture is important. If a counselee has never done so

Psalm 119:16

before God, while you should not push him into a rash vow, it would be well to encourage him to make the sort of declaration that the Psalmist does, if he sincerely intends to carry it out. Commitments like this can make all the difference in how one carries on in the future. It is important for every Christian to do regular Bible study; one cannot get it all in church services.

GIMEL

17 Grant to your servant that I may live and I will keep Your Word.

The word **grant** means "to confer a benefit upon." The wording may sound suspiciously like the writer is bargaining with God: "If you do so-and-so, then I'll do such and such." There are counselees who try such things. You cannot bargain with God. Make that clear to them. God sets forth His own terms which we accept or reject; we have neither the right nor the power to negotiate. Well then, what is the Psalmist saying? Simply this: "Confer upon me what is necessary to live and keep Your Word." He is asking for help. He is asking God to enable him to do what He requires of him in the Bible. He knows that he isn't able to do this by his own strength, so he is asking for the wisdom and the ability needed to accomplish what God has already laid down as commandments that he should keep. It takes time to learn both God's requirements and how to pull them off. He is praying for all that is necessary to make life abundant, meaningful, worthwhile. (Cf. Luke 24:32, 45.)

If a counselee is failing to do those things that God requires, if his life is dreary and unfruitful, then along

Psalm 119:18

with all else that he must do in counseling help him to learn how to rely on the Lord for all that he needs to accomplish that work. As a matter of fact, prayer of the sort that we encounter in this verse might be given to him as a homework assignment (see *The Christian Counselor's Manual* for details on giving homework). You could even tell him to use verse 17 for that purpose.

**18 Open my eyes that I may behold
Wonderful things out of Your law.**

Once more, refer to Luke 24:32 and 45. How little we know of God's Word! This is a prayer that cries out, "Let me see more!" The word **wonderful** refers to things that cause wonder, that amaze. Ask your counselee, "When you study the Scriptures are you amazed over and over by what you read—or have you lost your sense of wonder?" That is an important matter. If he says that he doesn't wonder any longer that is a danger signal. This loss of wonder may be the result of any one or more of several different factors. Perhaps he is in some sin that keeps him from Bible study. D. L. Moody wrote in the flyleaf of his Bible, "Either this Book will keep me from sin or sin will keep me from this Book." He was correct. Perhaps your counselee has never studied deeply enough to discover new and fascinating truth. Possibly he _____ (you fill in the blank). But whatever the problem, one of your objectives in counseling ought to be to help restore that sense of wonder that the counselee had when he first became a Christian and began to understand Scripture for the first time. J. A. Alexander reads the verse this way: "uncover my eyes and I will look." He sees the problem as a covering over the eyes that needs to be removed. Truly sin blinds. The verse, then, is asking God to remove whatever it is that keeps one from recognizing the won-

Psalm 119:19

ders of the Bible. The problem is not, as many seem to think, with the Bible; it is with them. Make that clear to the counselee who sees little or nothing wondrous in it.

The idea in this verse is connected closely with that in verse 10. There is great desire to learn the Bible when one discovers **wonderful things** in it. You might describe this sense of wonderment as similar to that of a child who is just beginning to discover what is in this world in which he lives. Indeed, the child of God is just that—a child in spiritual things—no matter how advanced his understanding may be. He too should marvel as he explores the wonderland of biblical truth! If the counselor handles the Word of God with joy and wonder, making it clear how he views its contents, he is likely to communicate something of the spirit of this verse to his counselees. He should, as well, be able to produce **things** from the Bible that incite wonder in the counselee.

**19 I am a stranger in the earth;
Don't hide your commandments from me.**

Of course, there is the possibility that he has a different problem. Because God **hides** His truth from those who fail to appreciate it. Studying it or trying to put it into practice, in that attitude, may blind one to it. God will not have His precious Word trampled under foot like a pig would trample pearls. In this regard, compare also Luke 8:17 and 18. One may even lose what little he has gained if he fails to act on what he has learned.

The Psalmist recognized that he was traveling in a foreign land and needed a road map. The commandments of God alone can guide one in the right way to go. Tell your counselee that though he is without friends or home in this world of sin, he can get along properly, if he seeks help from God in the Scriptures. For the stability necessary, God has given all that is needed in Scripture .

There are times when counselees themselves express the idea that they seem a **stranger** to all around. They talk of having no friends or of the fact that no one understands. When a counselee talks like that it is time to refer him to this verse. "If you seem a stranger, then here is how God expects a stranger to act—he should keep close to the Bible." That will be his sufficient guide.

**20 My soul breaks in longing
For Your judgments at all times.**

The Bible ought to be a constant companion; one that is ever at hand. And the Christian's desire to know more and more of it ought not to come and go with the seasons. He ought always, under every circumstance, to be anxious to hear what God's **judgments** of various matters may be. Nor should one think it possible to put off turning to the Bible in times of need, times of joy—when things are going badly or when they are going well. One ought to look on the Scriptures as important to *everything* that he does in life. Too often one's interest in the study of Scripture is sporadic. He studies when he is "in the mood." There are times when interest is born of excitement or need; at other times interest is nil.

The idea that one's **soul is breaking** means not so much that it is cracking up or crushed as that it is being rubbed away, wearing thin, close to the breaking point. Probably the best indication of this problem is when one is continually frustrated in his attempts to achieve something. It is then, through that period, that he may rely on the Word to comfort, sustain and guide him. It will do so *continually*. He may rely on it **at all times.**

Psalm 119:21

**21 You have rebuked the proud who are cursed,
Who wander from Your commandments.**

The proud of this world are those who fail to humble themselves before God and His Word. Certainly professed atheists fit this category, but so too do some professing Christians who handle God's Word in such a way that, at times, one wonders if they have not **wandered** so far from it that they belong among the **cursed** ones. They are the new liberals in the "evangelical" fold. They question the Bible much in the way that the old liberals did—finding contradictions, errors, myth, etc. They adopt a type of form criticism that is nearly akin to the old liberalism. It is they that one must fear more than the old liberals who have little influence today. Counselors must be careful not to become too closely associated with this crowd. It is they who most strongly advocate bringing in psychologies that are incompatible with biblical principles. Too often the idea behind what they teach seems to be that since the Bible isn't all that trustworthy a guide for life, let's turn to psychology to enhance it.

Pride goes before a fall (Proverbs 16:18). God will **rebuke** all those who tamper with His Word. It is the essence of pride for any counselor—or anyone else—to think he is *above* the Bible. There are various ways in which one may assume that unenviable position. He may criticize the Bible. He may act as if he has every aspect of Scripture in hand. He may meddle with various passages, conjecturing what the original might have said, etc. But if he does any of these things, or anything similar, he may be sure that in one way or another God will severely rebuke him. He even speaks of such persons being **cursed**. That is serious; indeed, it is very heavy language. The proper way for a counselor to use the Bible is as that

Word from God which is so superior to him that it determines and guides him in all that he does. He must see himself *beneath* it. He must see the Bible as ruling over him rather than he as ruling over it. Maintain the proper attitude toward God and His Word and don't **wander** from either.

**22 Remove reproach and scorn from me
Since I have kept Your testimonies.**

The word **remove** is, literally, "roll off." He sees **reproach and scorn** as a heavy burden from which he needs relief. The load of false accusations, gossip and slander that he has been carrying is too much for him. On the basis that he has kept God's testimonies, he asks for this relief. The Psalmist is not saying that he deserves anything from God, but he does remind God of His many gracious promises to bless those who live according to His Word. He therefore appeals to the heavenly Father for more grace.

God will bless those who do His will as it is set forth in the Bible. You can expect slander and scorn, however, when you adhere to Scriptural ways. Counselees should be alerted to that fact. When they do God's will they can expect others to persecute them. But you must understand that God's Word will sustain in the midst of it all and that, according to His promises, He will lift the burdens in His time (cf. I Corinthians 10:13). The next verse shows how large the burden was; it involved not merely private persons, but also rulers who plotted against him.

Psalm 119:23

**23 Princes also sat and spoke against me,
But Your servant meditated on Your
statutes.**

Here, persons of authority and power are pictured as sitting in judgment about the Psalmist. There is injustice being shown to him. But instead of dwelling on these things, he turns to the Bible and **meditates** on it (see v. 15). How important to give similar advice to counselees. A boss, or someone of importance in his life, is falsely accusing, slandering or otherwise plotting to get rid of your counselee for no just reason. Where should he turn to find help in such troublesome times? To the Bible, of course. Not to people, but to God in His Word. Instill that concept in the mind of counselees and you will have done them as much good as anything you could say to them in counseling. Why? What will the Bible do under such circumstances? The next verse makes that clear:

**24 Your testimonies also are my delight and my
counselors.**

Ultimately, you are not a counselor. God is the only Counselor. He counsels through His Word. Your task is to be able to point your counselees to that counsel in the Bible. But it is the Bible itself that actually provides the counsel. You are a sort of guide to *the* Guide, a friend of the Bridegroom, as John the Baptist put it. You have the privilege of helping His people come to God in His Word to find what is necessary in times of need and trouble. That is why you should **delight** in God's **testimonies**. You have what no other counselor has. You have an infallible, inerrant Source of truth to which you may turn for the proper counsel for your counselees. Can you imagine any counselor **delighting** himself in the words of Freud or

Psalm 119:23

Maslow? The idea is absurd (or, if it should actually happen, perverse!). But to be able to turn to the counsel of the loving God, the One Who created and sustains human beings—well, there is something truly to **delight** one's self in.

In the original Hebrew, the verse reads "men of my counsel." Turning to the Bible is a matter of turning to those inspired men who gave us God's counsel. It is as if you could consult with Isaiah, David, Paul or John to obtain the inerrant counsel of God. What a difference from seeking the "counsel of the ungodly." Here, it is seeking the counsel of God from His godly ones! If you don't appreciate what you have as your source of truth fully enough to **delight** in God's counsel, then it is time to discover why. Are you mixing it with the counsel of men? Are you not digging deeply into the Bible so as to ascertain exactly what God is saying in any given passage? Is it because you have "bought into" some of the neo-evangelical approaches to Scripture? What is wrong? As a biblical counselor, the Scriptures continually ought to be your **delight**. Perhaps there is sin in your life that is clouding your vision of the wondrous things in God's law. Possibly you, yourself, need to heed the counsel of the Word in some respect. Whatever the problem, get to the bottom of it. If counselees need to encounter anything when they come to counseling, they should encounter a counselor who thoroughly enjoys—indeed, **delights** in—the Bible. Nothing short of that will create the truly biblical counseling atmosphere and context necessary to do effective counseling.

Psalm 119:25

DALETH

**25 My soul clings to the dust;
Give me life according to Your Word.**

The Psalmist is in danger of dying. Counselees sometimes face death, sometimes have loved ones who are doing so. This is a verse for them. He is cast down and begs for restoration. He sees himself **clinging** (adhering to, glued to) **the dust** of the earth. Probably, this expression is reminiscent of Genesis 3:19. Even in death—or near death—one may find help in the Bible. Indeed, where else would he find help? In a hospice? Well, there may be physical comfort there. In friends? Well, there may be warmth of fellowship there. But where would he find that encouragement which will enable him to withstand the rigors of near death or death itself other than in the Bible? Why is that so? Because it is here also that he may find **life**. If, according to God's promises in His Word, he is able to find the life-giving solution to his problem, he may be able to be restored to life. If not, to life above. Either way, it is **life** that the Bible holds forth for him. You, as a biblical counselor, clearly have something unique to offer! Who but a biblical counselor can offer life? What a Book!

**26 I have declared my ways and You heard me;
Teach me Your statutes.**

It could be that the Psalmist here speaks of God's response to the prayer in the previous verse. If not, he speaks of some similar situation. How does your counselee respond when God has provided the help he needed through biblical guidance? Does he then forget the Bible? Well, shouldn't he all the more delight in it and seek to

Psalm 119:27

know more of what it teaches? If it can restore to life, think about what else it can do. That is the Psalmist's response. He says, "I prayed earnestly, **declaring** all my ways to You, O Lord." Perhaps this involved the confession of sin. At the very least, it meant submitting all his ways to God for His observation and possible blue-penciling. He is not demanding that God accept his ways; he is asking God to take a look at them so as to alter whatever needs to be altered. One senses a note of submission to the will of God that rings through what he is saying. That is what counselees must likewise do. They must not be so entirely committed to what they want that they are unwilling to have God change their plans. Then when God hears and answers *His way*, the proper thing for a counselee to do is to thankfully, willingly acquiesce. Moreover, he should again search the Scriptures in order to know how to ascertain God's will for the future. There is much that he should have learned from the way in which God answered his prayer. If there are alterations to his plans, he must find out why God made those changes (if possible) in order to plan more carefully in days ahead. He will be able to discover such facts in the Bible alone. That is why the Psalmist says, **teach me Your statutes**.

**27 Make me understand the way of your
       precepts,
   And I will meditate on your wonders.**

To **meditate** here means to talk to yourself. See verse 15. It is to tell one's self over and over again all that God has done. It is to look at God's **wondrous** deeds from every angle so as to appreciate and relate them to one's life. It is God's wonderful providence that is in view. The Bible provides abundant data for meditation; it gives one something to think and talk about.

Psalm 119:28

The request is for **understanding**. Too many counselees are willing to go along with only a modicum of understanding of the Bible. They do not own a concordance, a Bible Dictionary or a single commentary. They are not serious about their Bible study. They spend their time, if they do anything, filling in blank spaces in so-called "Bible study guides" that only promote poor interpretation by means of sharing ignorance. If one prays for **understanding**, it is necessary for him to follow up that prayer by doing those things that procure understanding. Counselees need to be instructed about this matter.

**28 My soul is dropping with grief;
Strengthen me according to Your Word.**

There is no doubt that counselees can grow weak through grief. It can wear one away like rain dripping on a roof. Biblical grief (grief with hope) is appropriate in the death of a loved one (cf. I Thessalonians 4:13ff). But there are those who continue to mourn as if there were no hope. There will be counselees who are heavy with grief who are grieving over other losses as well. Many grieve over the loss of a divorced spouse, the loss of a wayward child, the loss of a job or home, etc. Grief, if continued, unabated, will wear one down and even destroy health. It is therefore crucial to find the strength that is needed in the Scriptures. The Bible alone has facts about life and death that one may depend upon. Words of consolation from others may only irritate. But God has answers, has comfort, has encouragement. Moreover, in His Word, He teaches how to bear up under grief. If counselees are not finding their way out of grief after a reasonable time following the loss, it is time to challenge them with biblical teaching, some of which has to do with refocusing one's concern from himself to others.

**29 Remove the way of lying from me,
And graciously grant me Your law.**

Any number of counselees find it hard to tell the truth. They are liars. When it becomes clear that you have a counselee who has been lying to others, to you, etc., it is important for him to repent and confess this sin to all involved. He must then seek help from God in overcoming this sinful habit. The Word of God will give him all the help he needs. An exposition of Ephesians 4:25, as it applies to his life, showing how others depend upon his telling the truth, would be one way in which to discover how the Bible contains the answer to his prayer. And, as we have already seen, it is not enough to ask God to help without taking the biblical steps to bring about that help. You pray for your daily bread, but you work for it too! God works in and through the ways set forth in His Word. **Removing** lying also involves cutting off the right foot, hand, etc.—whatever it is that has led to lying in the past—eliminating it from one's life. He must remove every known temptation to sin that he can. It is a matter of learning to become a truth-teller in those situations in which one has previously learned to prevaricate.

God does **graciously** grant this request when made sincerely by His people. It is not true that once a counselee has become a liar he will always be a liar. If a spouse, or anyone else, says so, he must be challenged. Rather, he may put lying behind him once and for all. There is all sorts of hope in this verse for those who have become habituated (not addicted) to lying. Don't let counselees talk to you about the "need to lie" as some do today. That is the language of excuse. There is no "need." Lying is of the devil, who is called in Scripture the great deceiver, the father of lies. When one lies, he is taking his

Psalm 119:30

stand with Satan. Tell counselees that. Warn them of the danger of lying and help them to come to the place where they too utter this prayer.

**30 I have chosen the way of truth;
I have laid out Your judgments before me.**

The way one goes is a matter of **choice**. Even if one drifts into his lifestyle, as many do, that too is a choice—a choice not to make a choice. As he **laid out** God's judgments before him, the writer of this Psalm was able to discern what was the way of truth. Then, he could choose it. That is what so many don't do; they fail to look at the biblical data in order to choose rightly. Instead, they rely on hunches, feelings, "promptings" and the like, about which the Bible gives not a single hint. When you lay out a tray of rings in a jewelry store, for instance, that enables you to choose from various options the ring you prefer. That is how one should make choices about life-decisions. The Bible sets forth two **ways**: God's way, and all others. Both are described. It is clear when they are **laid out** before one, then compared and contrasted, which is which. Counselors must set forth the alternatives from the Bible. That is one of their principal tasks. No one *drifts* **into** truth; it must be **chosen.**

**31 I have clung to Your testimonies;
Yahweh, don't shame me.**

Too many persons who come for counseling are there because they have let go of truth. God commands, "Buy the truth and sell it not" (Proverbs 23:23). Here is the statement of one who **clung** to truth for all he was worth. There are so many siren voices today that would lure one into a different path. The TV, the Internet, the daily news on radio and in the paper, magazines, films, all send forth a message that, in the end, is false. They try to lure people into the ways of unrighteousness. Sometimes this is done consciously; in other instances, it is not. Many don't even know (or care) about what is righteous or unrighteous. They simply advocate that which pleases them or which, for some reason or other, they think is correct. They, of course, have no standard of truth and righteousness. As a result, they become their own standard. They follow the old (false) dictum: "To thyself be true." There is no reason why anyone who clings to God's truth should be put to **shame**. In the face of his enemies and detractors he ought to be able to triumph rather than be embarrassed by defeat. That is, of course, what the Psalmist is talking about.

**32 I will run the way of Your commandments
When You will enlarge my heart.**

When it comes to obeying God's **commandments**, God doesn't countenance those who take a lackadaisical stroll. He prefers those who **run** to do His will. "If only You will expand my capacity to understand and do what You say, Lord," says the writer, "I will speedily do what You tell me to do." The **heart** is the inner you. It is what you really are like, what you think, what you believe, what you know. Probably, most Christians seem to know more than they actually do. They pretend to be more astute than they are. But here is one who admits his need for a greater ability to understand. Counselees who do likewise will surely be given what they request: God will expand their ability to learn and do as He directs. How important, then, to come to God honestly, with a heart that is anxious to be **enlarged**.

Psalm 119:33

He

**33 Yahweh, teach me the way of Your statutes,
And I will keep it to the end.**

Again, there is the *desire to learn*. That, of course, is the prerequisite to doing so. Without this heartfelt desire it seems futile to even talk about the Word of God. If people lack that desire, they will not learn. However, learning God's way means learning to *observe* (cf. Matthew 28:18-20). That is what the Psalmist refers to when he says that he will **keep it** [the way of God] **to the end**. It is learning to do, learning to live.

Counselees will tell you that we need no instruction in the way of sin. That comes from simply drifting. G. K. Chesterton said that "The only Christian doctrine that is provable is the doctrine of original sin!" But, though each new believer is weighted toward sin by his learned behavior, the Lord (**Yahweh**) is the Greatest Teacher. He, by His Spirit, can **teach** what to do and how to do it—both aspects of the instruction that are needed. He weighs heavier than any habit, no matter how long it has persisted. Your counselee should, with the Psalmist, cry out for Yahweh to instruct him. (Cf. the pointed verse in John 6:45!)

He says that once having learned God's **way**, he will **keep it to the end**. He will persist, literally, "to the heel." That is, to the extremity. To the farthest point. The biblical way that God directs, once learned, will be the way that he will walk throughout the rest of his life. He will persevere in the truth. The word for **teach** here means "to throw, to cast." It has the idea of throwing it down in front of the student. In Christ's school, there is little that is indirect about His teaching; what He said was not said "in a corner." He puts it up front, as we would say; "throws it down in front of," as the writer put it. In other words, it is not something for a special group, some esoteric doctrine fitted to a small group. No, it is for every believer alike. Therefore, never allow a counselee to protest that he isn't of the sort who can study and understand. Ask him, "When the Bible says 'Believe and be saved,' isn't that simply spreading out the truth before you? Isn't it simply thrown down without embellishment? Is it so difficult?" And for those who believe, God says, "Honor your father and mother." Ask him, "What is so difficult about comprehending that?" In other words, the **way** that God requires your counselee to go is chalked out in the Bible; all one need do is follow it.

Certainly, there are portions more difficult than others, but the basic Christian life is clearly thrown down in front of every believer. All he need do is look at it. And the rest is readily understood, using basic Bible helps, by those who become genuine students of Scripture.

34 Make me understand and I will keep Your law
And observe it with my whole heart.

The word for **understanding** comes from the Hebrew *bin* which has in it the idea of dividing between things, or discerning. There is little discernment in the church today. People accept much of the biblically unsubstantiated puff that is offered on the radio and in Christian bookstores today as if it were gospel, when so much of it is, at best, frightfully wrong. The need for discernment, distinguishing truth from error, is what the Psalmist is praying for. Perhaps your counselee is in trouble precisely because he bought into some bad teaching. He needs to learn discernment. Discernment, as the writer of Hebrews

Psalm 119:35

made clear, comes from the understanding and habitual use of the Scriptures (cf. Hebrews 5:14; see my book *A Call for Discernment* for additional help).

The Psalmist speaks of **keeping** God's **law** with his **whole heart**. We have encountered this before, and we shall encounter it again. There is recognition in this phrase of the need to be "sold out" to God. One cannot have a foot on two paths that diverge widely from one another. Some who fall into trouble do so because that is their strategy. They want God's way, but they don't want to abandon other ways as well. Counselors who take this stance with reference to using Scripture *and* psychology find themselves encouraging counselees to do this. If you believe you can counsel biblically and some other way at the same time, you will only set a poor example for counselees.

**35 Make me walk in the path of Your
      commandments
      Because I delight in it.**

We have commented before that God's **way** is a **delight**. Now that fact is urged as a motive for **walking** in it. Who is it who doesn't want to do what he considers a **delight**? Well, then, what keeps Christians from walking in God's **path**? One factor—they fail to consider doing so a **delight**. When counselees protest about following biblical directives, they need to be brought up short about this matter. "You mean you don't simply delight in doing what God here commands?" In many cases, the answer will be, "Of course, I don't delight in doing it; it's hard." Then read this verse. The problem is not merely to do what God says, but to come to view doing it in an entirely different way. *There* is where the counselor must concentrate his efforts. He must help the counselee to **delight** in serving and pleasing God.

One must not be coerced into biblical action. The act itself may be hard and unpleasant, but every counselee must do what God says *in order to please Him.* And that ought to be his *desire.* Persecution is not desirable; one should not desire it. But suffering persecution, when need be, *for Christ's sake,* should be *desired.* The pleasures of sin are in the doing; the pleasures of righteousness are in the result (cf. Hebrews 11:24-27). Perhaps, counselor, if you are having trouble getting counselees to obey the plain requirements of the Bible, it is because they are not motivated by a desire to please their heavenly Father, and therefore, have no **delight** in righteous behavior.

**36 Bow my heart to Your testimonies
And not to unjust gain.**

Here we leave generalities and turn to a specific request: to have the **heart bow** down to the Bible so as to not worship money and stoop to dishonest practices to obtain it. The heart may be full of ambition and covetousness. It needs to be broken of this willfulness and bow before the commandments of the Scripture that teach against obtaining money **unjustly**. Many counselees have fallen prey to this problem. They have lived for money instead of for the Lord. They have adopted and followed the sharp practices of the world rather than walking the line chalked out in the Bible about honesty in money-making. Here is a powerful verse to use with them, in conjunction with the passages in I Timothy 6. The combination should get results.

But the concept of **bowing** is important in this context. One cannot serve two masters: God and Mammon (literally, one's "pile" [of money]). It is a matter of wor-

Psalm 119:37

ship; as Paul said, "Covetousness. . . is idolatry" (Colossians 3:5). Will you **bow** to the Word (in effect, by this, bowing to God) or to money? Put that way, counselees may be brought to repentance and make changes appropriate to it. If one becomes a Christian and that doesn't make any changes in his business life, there is something wrong. A good question to ask of counselees is: "How has the Bible changed the way you do business (or the way you handle money)?"

Incidentally, there is no bibliolatry in this verse; one is bowing in submission to God when he bows to His testimonies.

**37 Turn my eyes from looking at vanity;
In Your way give me life.**

There is danger in watching sin, as Psalm 1 makes clear. The one who walks toward it may soon be standing fascinated by it, eventually to be sitting in the place of those who advocate it. The emptiness [**vanity**] of the way of life portrayed on TV is apparent to any Christian who is even minimally acquainted with it. There is not much worth viewing. It is dangerous to fill one's mind with the philosophies underlying the dramas and the other fare served up. One must be very conscious of what is going on in order not to be caught up in the non-Christian ways that are glamorized. Counselor, this should be the modern TV "addict's" prayer!

Rather than center his interests and attention on vain things, the Christian should spend his time endeavoring to walk in God's **way**. It is the place to find the abundant **life**. The emptiness and vanity of the one lifestyle over against the fullness and meaningfulness of the other is what the Psalmist is contrasting. Make the contrast clear to counselees whose problem is what they spend their time viewing. This is clearly a problem of the "eyegate," as Bunyan called it in his story about the invasion of Mansoul.

**38 Make sure Your Word to Your servant
Who wants to fear You.**

That is to say, confirm it. Many counselees are skeptical about what God says. They wonder whether they have understood correctly, because they do not seem to receive the outcomes of their prayers that they thought they should. Sometimes this is because they were wrong in their expectations. The Word is confirmed to such people by clarifying what it teaches, and therefore what proper expectations they should have. Sometimes they want what they want when *they* want it, rather than to wait for God (see verses on waiting in Psalm 25). What they expect is proper because it accords with the Word. They need to be confirmed in their trust in the Word by showing them this, but also by making it plain that God's watch runs on a different timetable than ours ("a thousand years is as a day" with Him).

Some discouraged, downhearted, dispirited counselees simply need to get things straight so that their trust in the Bible does not waver. The **fear** of God is dependent, as the verse indicates, on one's certain trust in what He says in the Bible. The way to confirm one's shaken faith, then, is to shore up one's understanding of the Bible.

This means that, in cases of this sort, you must get to the heart of the misinterpretation or misapplication of biblical passages. It also means that you must be able to give a proper interpretation and make a proper application of them. That is why every counselor must constantly study his Bible in a serious, exegetically-oriented manner. He

Psalm 119:39

must be able to correct the gainsayers who may have rocked the faith of his counselee, and must be able to help him to see things clearly.

Much popular Christian literature today is calculated to cause problems for your counselees. Magazines present "two views of. . ." articles. Books, with titles like "Four views of the. . ." are prevalent. An author (or editor) ought to state his view plainly, why he believes it and why other opposing views are wrong. In books presenting "Four views," at least three of them are wrong. Why present on the open market a book, three fourths of which one knows from the outset contains error? That is not the way in which Paul, Peter or our Lord taught.

**39 Turn away my reproach which I fear;
Your judgments are good.**

Reproach (or "shame") will come to all who stand for truth. The world is in the business of trying to silence the truth by such methods. It cannot stand the light in its presence. So it tries to put out the light by slander, ostracism, making fun of it, etc. A believer ought not to succumb to this attack. That, of course, is exactly what the Psalmist **fears**. The last thing that he wants to do is to misrepresent the truth of God and bring shame on it by his lifestyle. He should not **fear** what many say, but fears that he might; if he does and hides his light under a bushel, he brings reproach on the Word of God. God's **judgments are good**. That is what he wants to maintain in word and what he wants to demonstrate in deed. He fears he may back down on that appraisal or on his advocacy of it. Counselors will deal with those who are suffering from this malady. Help encourage them to stand fast.

**40 See! I have longed for Your precepts;
     In Your righteousness give me life.**

Compare with verse 20. The Psalmist wants to do as God wishes; that is his **longing**, or great desire. To do as he should, he thinks he needs joy, energy, vigor (here expressed in the word **life**). It is true that doing the things God commands with life is the way He wants us to act. But one should go ahead and act, all the while praying for vigor to pursue the will of God, and (in the doing) he will discover that the strength and vigor will come. He should not sit around waiting for it. God **gives** abundant **life** to those who demonstrate that they truly wish to serve Him.

VAV

**41 Let Your lovingkindnesses come to me,
     Yahweh,
     According to Your salvation, according to
     Your Word.**

The **lovingkindnesses** of God are His gracious acts toward men. The word is roughly equivalent to the New Testament term "grace." Here the Psalmist is asking that the grace of God that flows from **salvation** be given to him, and that it be given in accordance with the promises found in His **Word**. No counselee could ask for more. Indeed, if more counselees had asked earlier for God's promised grace, they probably would not now need to come for counseling. It is, however, important to note that what he asks for is not that his own desires be met, not that his terms be accepted. What the counselee, following these words, should request of Yahweh is that those graces that God has promised to give the heirs of **salva-**

Psalm 119:42

tion be granted him. In other words, he is asking for nothing other than that which God has already made clear He is willing to do for His people. There is the hitch. Because counselees don't know God's **Word** adequately, 1) they may fail to ask for enough; 2) they may ask amiss; 3) they may not even know what to ask for. Once more, the importance of knowing Scripture is underlined.

Counselors should be able to point to these biblical promises, set them forth with assurance, and urge counselees to pray and act in accordance with them. If counselees demand that which God has *not* promised in the Bible, they also ought to be ready to point this out and to suggest proper biblical alternatives. For instance, if God has not promised to deliver His people from distress immediately upon asking for it, a counselor should point out those passages that indicate He *eventually* will do so, and in the meanwhile, will sustain the counselee in his trials (I Corinthians 10:13).

How many counselees spend their time complaining rather than imploring God for a visitation of His lovingkindnesses?

**42 And I will have a word for the one who
    accuses me,
    Since I trust in Your Word.**

The word translated **accuse** means to vilify. It could speak either of informal accusations or those that are brought forward in a law court. Either way, the Psalmist is encouraging your counselee, who probably faces accusations in an informal situation (though not necessarily), to be able to respond in accordance with Scripture. In every area of life (formal or informal) the believer ought to be able to justify his words and conduct by Scripture. That is true even if he has sinned. In such cases, he ought to be

Psalm 119:43

able to show that he has repented and done works that the Bible requires of sinning believers appropriate to repentance. At no point, then, is a Christian free from following the Bible.

When he is reproached, vilified, **accused** (all of which actions are encompassed in this large Hebrew term), in answer to those who inquire about his response, he ought to be able to prove that he has done the responsible, biblical thing required of him. Moreover, he will also have a proper response (**word**) to give his accuser, if it is in line with biblical principles (for example, those in Romans 12:14-21). How vital is the Bible in daily living in a sinful world. The Christian who knows the Scriptures, and who lives according to them, ought never to be at loss as to what to say when accused by another. If he is guilty of the accusation, his response is not to cover up, but to confess his sin, seek forgiveness and to change. If not guilty, he should be able to respond to his accuser in the right attitude, proving that the accusation falls short of the mark. Either way, he ought to be able to handle accusations as no non-Christian can.

**43 And take not the word of truth entirely from my mouth,
Since I have hoped in Your judgments.**

By comparison see Psalm 45:1 and 2. This verse is speaking about the need to stand up for **truth** when necessary. The Psalmist wants to be able to respond as he should in such times. He wants to be a witness for the **truth**. He dreads the possibility of failing to speak when he should—as if the **word of truth** (in a situation when error is being propagated, for instance) had been completely removed from his **mouth**. The need to have the courage to speak God's **truth** is what is in view. Too

Psalm 119:44

often, out of fear, counselees hesitate to say what they know ought to be said. Parents fear to tell children what they need to hear. Members of the church become tongue-tied (as we would put it) when they ought to encourage one another through rebuke or counsel. There is far too much hesitancy to speak God's truth; it is almost as if His people were ashamed to say what they think. Here is the verse to counteract fearful hesitancy of that sort. John 17:17 also refers to the fact that God's **Word** is **truth**.

If one truly **hopes** in God's judgments, he should be able to talk about them. The biblical term **hope** doesn't mean "hope so," as our modern term does. It means, rather, a confident expectation (or anticipation) of the fulfillment of God's promises. The certainty of what God has promised is not in question. The only factor that makes hope hope is that the promise has not yet been realized. The fulfillment of it is as certain as if it were history. This kind of hope (which a non-Christian counselor can never offer his counselees) is what makes Christian counseling so exciting. The counselor *knows* that if one does as God says, the results that God promises are inevitable. God cannot lie! He therefore can assure counselees of the outcome of certain actions. Because that is true, counselees also ought to be able to speak with confidence, not be hesitant out of fear.

**44 And I shall keep Your law continually—
Forever and ever.**

The number of verses beginning with **and** in this section is due to the fact that there are so few other words in Hebrew that begin with the letter *vav*. They do not indicate continuation of a thought from one verse to another.

Here is a life-commitment to observing the commandments of God. How wonderful if this were the com-

Psalm 119:45

mitment of every Christian! Certainly it would aid counseling if, apart from coercion, counselees would reach this determination. It is a verse that every counselor may hold before his counselees. But it is also one that he ought to have in *his* mind at all times. With reference to his counseling, how important that he should be willing to commit himself to the use of God's word in counseling as long as he is able to counsel! He will not allow the fashions of the time, etc., to draw him away from the Bible. That is one way in which he may **keep** God's law, as it is required of him, for instance, in Psalm 1, which tells him to avoid the "counsel of the ungodly" and to meditate day and night in the Bible. When counselees see that their counselor adheres strictly to the Bible in his counseling, they too are more likely to do so. Indeed, if a counselor has made such a life-commitment, he might even mention it at an appropriate point in counseling.

**45 And I will walk in a broad place
Since I seek Your commands.**

What God's **commandments** do for a Christian is to *enlarge* his thinking and his lifestyle—not shrink and restrict it, as the world seems to think. He is restrained from evil so as to free him for doing good (cf. Romans 6, 7). Because the unbeliever may not experience the joys of salvation and its effects on one's way of life, he has no idea about how greatly one's viewpoint is enlarged by thinking God's thoughts after Him. A young person who becomes a Christian and leaves the drug culture behind can testify to how drugs limited him, and how his new life has freed him for far more productive living.

Many Christians, however, fail to recognize this fact and they, themselves, have a jaundiced idea about the keeping of God's **commandments**. They often echo the

Psalm 119:45

non-Christian view that Christianity narrows rather than **broadens**. It is a counselor's privilege to counter this idea by showing how following the Bible in any given circumstance will lead to freedom and greater expression of one's potential. That is something you as a counselor ought to be prepared to do all of the time.

A wife says, "If I submit to my husband, then I will lose many of my freedoms." How would you respond to that statement in the light of this verse? Think about it and write out your answer in the space below.

Then, write out about three other such objections that you have heard Christians make, together with your responses to them. Once you get the hang of it, you will be prepared to deal with all such objections. Write out those objections and your responses in the space following:

1

2

3

Don't fail to notice also that in this verse the writer **seeks** to learn and do God's commands. That means that they are not being forced upon him. He willingly does them, with a desire to find the ways in which this enlargement of his lifestyle may take place. As a matter of fact, once you have made the point from this verse (and v. 96) you may also give a counselee the assignment of writing

Psalm 119:46

out ways in which following specific commandments that relate to his situation will *enlarge* his **walk**.

**46 And I will speak of Your testimonies before kings,
And I will not be ashamed.**

This verse might fruitfully be used in conjunction with verse 43, upon which I have commented already. It is the counterpart to the sentiment expressed there. When one has the word of truth in his mouth (on the tip of his tongue, we would say) he is unashamed of it, and will speak of God's truth wherever he may be—even in the highest circles. Your counselee probably will not have the opportunity to speak in the presence of kings, but he will often have occasion to speak to various authorities who hold some power over him. He should not fear to "speak the truth in love" on such occasions. If a counselee is anticipating doing so with trepidation, especially if he is uncertain about how to do so, a wise counselor might role play the occasion with him until he begins to "get it right."

Daniel, the apostle Paul, and others have literally fulfilled this word. We read of their faithfulness in the Bible as an encouragement to us. They were not supermen; they were men of "like passions with us," who had the same fears and trepidations that we do. Yet God strengthened them to speak His Word. He will do the same for your counselee in his time of testing. Never hesitate to encourage counselees to **speak God's testimonies**—but always be as sure as you can be that they know *what* to say and *how* to say it. And be sure that they talk to the Lord about it as this Psalmist did.

Psalm 119:47

**47 And I will delight in Your commandments,
Which I have loved.**

Here is a goal for every counselor and counselee: to reach the point in his Christian experience at which he can honestly say this to God. If one has been learning and doing what God commands, experiencing the enlarged vision and lifestyle that this provides, he will have every reason to **love** the Bible and to **delight** in perusing it further. Bible study and application to life should become a **delight**. How dreary for a Christian to know that in this Book is contained all that he needs for a life of joy and happiness, a life of freedom and opportunity, but neither to know what the Book says nor to be living according to it! Counselor, if you can open up the Word to him to see that this is what the Bible can do for him, and get him started in becoming a Bible **lover**, you will have done more to change his life than anything else you could ever do. It is not only the solution to specific problems with which a counselor should deal; rather, it is to create a **love** for, a **delight** in, doing more and more of God's will. Think about this. Put some time in planning how you will go about it in counseling. Draw up a definite plan for introducing this thought in each counseling case. What will you do? Write it out in the space below:

**48 And I will lift up my hands to Your
commandments which I have loved;
And I will meditate on Your statutes.**

Lifting up of the hands was a sign of joy. The Psalmist is saying that every time he came to understand and appreciate a **commandment**, he would rejoice over the fact. There is here an expression that, possibly, is most closely akin to our expression "I will take off my hat to . . . ." To do so is to salute someone or something. To lift up the hands *to* the commandments is, therefore, a sign of respectful joy. It doesn't mean lifting up hands in prayer. It means to so appreciate the statute that one must do something to acknowledge the fact.

Why is the Bible read, but not **meditated** on? Because it is not **loved**. Only one who has come to so appreciate it, as this verse describes him, will take the time to properly meditate on its truths and their application to his life. Only those who **love** God's **statutes** will spend the time and the effort to think of ways of *implementing* God's will expressed in Scripture. That is, of course, the result of sincere meditation (see v. 15 for more on meditation).

ZAYIN

49 Remember Your Word to Your servant
Upon which You have caused me to hope.

Comments on **hope** mentioned under verse 43 are also apropos here. The **Word** on which the Psalmist has come to hope is a word spoken **to** him. God's promises in the Bible are made not merely to those to whom they were first spoken; unless there is reason to believe they are special in application, they apply to you and your counselees as well (cf. Romans 15:4; I Corinthians 10:6, 11). There is every reason to ask God to fulfill His promises to His people. *How* He will do so, and *when*, may be uncertain, unless He has clearly stated something along those lines, but *that* He will do so is absolutely certain.

Psalm 119:50

It is interesting that the Psalmist says that God **caused** (or "made") him to **hope**. There should be no question about what God wants us to do; He is in the business of **causing** us to hope. That means that if a counselee comes doubting, wondering about, or trashing hope, there must be something wrong with his relationship to God. It is absolutely right to call him to hope (the biblical meaning of which is "to expect") that God will fulfill all His promises. Perhaps he has been a double-minded, rather than a *tam* or *teleios* person (cf. v. 1). James indicates that such a person will receive nothing from the Lord. One must truly depend upon God's Word if he expects to receive what God has promised. If he has no such hope, he ought to examine his life to discover what it is in which he is placing his hope rather than in God's Word. If he is trying to straddle the fence, to place hope both in Scripture and in something else, he needs to repent and ask God to **cause** him to hope as he should. There is nothing more certain than the promises of God in Scripture. Every counselee must hear that from his counselor in one form or another. If he doubts the truth of that statement, it is time to stop whatever else you are attempting to do and deal with that problem. After all, unless your counseling is based firmly on God's promises, you will get nowhere until both you and your counselee are agreed that is the thing to do. If he goes on trying to serve two masters—partially buying into God's promises and partially buying into something else—God will not hear him (James 1:7).

**50 This is my comfort in my affliction:
Since Your Word has given me life.**

The word **comfort** is a term applied to whatever "gives ease" in time of trouble or distress (cf. vv. 92, 71). The Psalmist recognizes that the real **comfort** that he

Psalm 119:51

obtains in time of trouble and affliction comes from God in His Word. You will read everywhere that it is *people* who bring **comfort**; the conventional wisdom is, "Counselor, in time of trouble, just to know that you are there is what is important." The most recent expression heard everywhere (often spoken rather meaninglessly) is "Just be there for me." Well, of course, some comfort comes from others; there is no doubt about that. But it is only supplementary, and it never heals, never lasts. It is particularly ineffective in times of death. And it is plain that when faced with the matter of death, Paul didn't suggest visiting and sitting like one of Job's counselors. No. That to which he pointed was his own words of Scripture: "Comfort one another with these words" (I Thessalonians 4:18). It is the words of Scripture that comfort; not the mute presence of friends. Remember that, would-be counselor.

When one is depressed, grieving, downcast from some affliction, it is the **Word** that brings new **life**. Friends are vital; but friends, counselors, ministers have one thing to do in such situations—present the appropriate biblical truth from God. Who but God the Spirit, taking His own Word, can reach into a troubled soul and give it new life?

**51 The proud have completely scorned me;
I have not deviated from Your law.**

Pride leads to scorning **and scoffing**. When one thinks he is above others, he tends to scorn those he thinks are beneath him. The more one swells with pride, the more he sees himself farther and farther above more and more others. Thus his scorning of others grows. It is sad to meet persons like that. From time to time you will encounter them in counseling. When you detect scornful

Psalm 119:52

attitudes on the part of a counselee, look for **pride**. Almost always you will discover that is at the bottom of the problem. This biblical connection between the two provides an important counseling insight.

When your counselee is the object of another's **scorn**, particularly when it is his Christian walk that is the butt of the proud scoffing, it is difficult for him to continue steadfast on a righteous path. It is easy to swerve. One does not appreciate being shamed or made fun of. That is particularly true when it is done in the sight of others. But the Psalmist does not concern himself with what others say or think. He says that when he was the object of scorn, it did not deter him; he would **not deviate** from God's **law**.

Sometimes one turns aside from living according to biblical commandments in such circumstances less from embarrassment than from wanting to strike back. He knows he should overcome evil with good (Romans 12:14ff.). Yet there is a temptation to **deviate** from the commandments in that passage and take vengeance into one's own hands. To deviate from God's law is to turn from the very truth that will help at such a time. It is, therefore, a foolish response. One must learn how to turn to the Bible on such occasions and adhere to its teachings all the more firmly. That is the advice counselees need.

**52 I remembered Your judgments from long
    ago, Yahweh,
    And comfort myself.**

Here, **remembering** what God has done and has said in times past makes all the difference to this Psalmist. And it should also to you and your counselees. But the one who needs comfort must make the effort to think back, to search out the words and works of God, and must

comfort himself with them. It is an active thing. It is not a matter of sitting around feeling sorry for one's self. That won't do. The reflexive action described in this verse implies effort on the part of the one who needs comforting. He does not merely sit and suffer; he doesn't expect others to console him. Rather, he gets busy and studies what God has said and done with reference to circumstances that accord to his. Then he finds the comfort that this provides. Advise such an active approach to affliction and trouble.

**53 I have been seized with a scorching horror
and indignation because of the wicked
Who forsake Your law.**

The mixture of hot **indignation and horror** that took hold of the Psalmist when he thought about the ways that wicked people turn from God's **law** was like the **scorching** blast of a sirocco wind. It brought anger over the act, but **horror** at the thought of what the end of those who did so would be. How does it affect you? Your counselee? It might be of interest to you to see what your counselee thinks about this matter—how he reacts. That will tell you something of his love for God and His Word. And also, something about his concern for the eternal welfare of those who despise and **forsake** the Bible.

If the fact doesn't shock you or him perhaps there is need to meditate on the holiness and the wrath of God. Those who truly **fear** God have a sense of terror mixed with detestation as they think about people deriding God's Word. They detest the attitude that such people take toward God by doing so, but at the same time they are terrified when they think of those same people having to face the holy God some day. If there is even a hint of a

Psalm 119:54

counselee **forsaking** the Bible, bring this verse to bear on him.

54 Your statutes have been songs
In the house of my travel.

When one is in a foreign land (the **house** of one's **travel**) he often sings or hums tunes that are familiar to him. These remind him of home. This world is the place where believers are strangers in a foreign land. We are traveling through a culture that is out of tune with ours. What will remind us of the fact? What will keep us yearning for our heavenly home (cf. Hebrews 11:13-16)? Why, the Scriptures, of course. Reciting them is like singing a familiar song that will cheer and comfort, that will encourage and guide.

55 In the night I have remembered Your Name,
 Yahweh,
 And have kept Your law.

The night is a time of danger. It is also a time for quiet reflection. In fear or in contemplation (though not necessarily discrete; the one may lead to the other) the place to turn is to God's **law**. The Name of God in view here is **Yahweh**, the ever-existing One. The One Who was, Who is, and Who will always be. He is the One Who has revealed this **Name** as His covenant Name. So whenever a counselee needs to be reminded that God has covenanted with him to save him through the Lord Jesus Christ, he ought to remember the name **Yahweh**. That is a marvelous thought to brighten a dreary, fretful **night**.

There are other meaningful names for God, each of which has its place in counseling. See my discussion of the principal names that counselors might find helpful in *The Christian Counselor's Manual*. A name of God speaks of His character and of His works. Those names are given to men for their instruction and benefit and should be used for that purpose.

**56 This was done to me
Because I kept Your commandments.**

What is he talking about? He is probably referring to all the beneficial things that God does through His Word that were mentioned in the previous seven verses. Once more, this remark stresses the value of **keeping** the requirements of God. Turning the verse inside out, think of all that God does to those who fail to keep His commandments!

The sentence is a summary statement, the need for which is important to understand. God does *many* good things for those who obey Him. It is not that God is stingy with His benefits. The Bible teaches that He *loads* us with them (Psalm 68:19). He is a God Who delights in blessing His children. It is important to make this clear to counselees who think God has neglected them. The fact is, either they fail to recognize and thank Him for His many blessings, or they fail to receive them because they don't **keep His commandments** as they should. If a counselee isn't receiving daily mercies from God (Lamentations 3:23), something is radically wrong. Talk to him about it. Investigate until you discover what is wrong.

CHETH

**57 Yahweh is my portion;
I have said that I will keep Your words.**

What a statement: **Yahweh is my portion!** What does he mean? The word **portion** refers to "something

Psalm 119:58

that one lays claim to." Many counselees want to own honor, wealth, fame, attention, pleasure, land, possessions; the Psalmist is excited to call **Yahweh** his own. To be able to lay claim to the Creator of the universe as one's own God—that is something. Yet it is true of all those who have through faith come to salvation. Why should problems stump one who can make such a claim? Remind the counselee who complains that he has so little of what he *does* have! Not only can he call God his portion, as over against those who lay claim to far less, but he can also call God his Savior, his Lord, his Master, his Shepherd. Most counselees who are down need to be boosted by remembering such facts. Then, in the light of the truth, they can forge ahead to do what is required of them, knowing that since God is *their* God He will be with them. Thank God for the possessive pronouns that he allows us to use with reference to Himself!

The phrase, **I have said**, is the upshot of the previous confession of God as one's **portion**. If He is—and He is—then there is no reason for not committing one's self to **keeping His Words**. In this verse, the statement, **I have said** is nothing less than a settled commitment. It is by making such a commitment that one is able to truly live the lifestyle that God requires of him. Call counselees to such a determined commitment.

**58 I looked for Your favor with my whole heart;
Show lovingkindness to me according to Your Word.**

To **look for** something is to *seek* it. Tonight, as I write, my son and his two boys have just told me that they are going out to "look for" Christmas presents. They don't look by simply sitting and expecting them to appear on their own. They don't expect someone to knock on the door and say, "Oh, glad you're home; I have the presents you want." No. They are going out into that shopping mob at the stores, in the mall—wherever—and will look and look and look until they find what they want. To look for God's lovingkindness will not take even that much effort, but it will take active work on the part of the counselee. He may not sit back and expect you to do everything for him. God's lovingkindness (grace) comes to the believer who asks for it, who looks in the Bible to see what God has for him in his circumstance. Grace is grace (**favor** undeserved), but one receives it when he looks for it.

**59 I thought about my ways
And turned my feet to Your testimonies.**

That, of course, is what counseling is all about—helping counselees to **think about their ways**. If they are discouraged, then they need to think about what led to that. How did they respond to some frustrating, disheartening happening? If a counselee is confused, then help him to consider what in his thinking led to that confusion. If he must make a decision, help the counselee to think about how he will make up his mind about the various options before him. A counselor is one who helps a counselee to consider his **ways**. He helps him think about how he responds to defeat. He helps him think about how he sizes up life's circumstances. He helps him to think about his attitudes, his words, his actions—all that he does.

But a biblical counselor does more. When he has helped him do that, he doesn't leave a counselee there—as many counselors must do. At best, they can give their opinion about how he might do otherwise, about how *he* thinks he ought to respond, how he should make deci-

Psalm 119:60

sions. Many, however, don't go even that far; they simply leave the matter up to him. The biblical counselor, having helped the counselee consider his ways, next helps him **turn to God's testimonies**. It isn't a matter of leaving him to fend for himself. It isn't a matter of saying, "Here are some alternatives; you'll have to decide which is the best one." It isn't even a matter of saying, "If I were you, here's what I'd do." No, the biblical counselor leaves nothing so indefinite. He helps the counselee to turn to the proper passages that deal with his situation to see what God says about it. He has him **think about his ways** in order to compare his ways with God's (cf. Isaiah 55:6-9). He helps him think through what he is doing that is in accord with Scripture and what is not. He then helps him to get back on the right track if he has gotten off. He helps him see how God wants him to make decisions. In short, the Christian counselor has a standard against which to measure a counselee's thought, attitude, words and behavior. He is not dealing in unknowns; he is dealing in *inerrant, revealed* truth. That makes all the difference.

**60 I hurried, and didn't delay,
     To keep Your commandments.**

The urgency in this verse is of note. It expresses what some counselees need to hear: obedience must not be put off. If one is involved in deciding whether to do God's will or not, there should be no **delay**. *Just as soon as he discerns God's will* he should decide to do it. It may take time to accomplish what is necessary. Fine, so long as that doesn't become a delaying tactic. It may take some further discussion with a counselor to know precisely how to do it. O.K. But to determine to do it should take no time at all. Then, he should do it just as soon as it is possible—even in a **hurry** so as to **keep God's commandments**.

"Can't I taper off on drugs?" one asks. Provided that as a counselor, you are working in tandem with a physician who says it is O.K. to come off now, there should be no delay. "Well, how about a little less each day?" Answer, "If you are going to cut a dog's tail you don't begin at the farthest point and make small slices until you reach the point where you want the cut to be." People want to break off their homosexual relationships gradually. No! That cannot be. In all such suggestions the focus is on the wrong person or persons. The counselee is thinking of himself, or he is thinking of his sexual paramour. Wrong! Look once more at the verse: the Psalmist is interested in **keeping** *God's* Word. The emphasis is on God, not self—or another. It is on obedience to God in order to please Him.

Having recognized this fact, counselor, say to your counselee something like this: "You mean to say that you are more concerned about how this change is going to affect you or your partner than you are about how it will affect God?" There is something wrong about that sort of thinking; it probably doesn't show true repentance. At the very best, it will show that one is extremely self-centered. He is willing to "taper *on*" his obedience to God! That is unacceptable. He should "flee" sin and temptation and **hurry** to God's way according to the Bible.

**61 The wicked's cords have surrounded me;
I have not forgotten Your law.**

It doesn't matter how tightly the world wraps its cords around me so as to draw me away, or to keep me from acting as I should, **I have not forgotten** God's **law**. That is what the Psalmist affirms. It doesn't matter how forcefully **wicked** persons may attempt to prohibit a counselee from doing God's will, he need not cave in. If

Psalm 119:62

he has learned what God desires him to be or do, and **remembers** it, he can thwart their best efforts. Danger, persuasion, threats—none of these things are stronger than the Word of God. Nor are the enticements of the world stronger than the love of Christ (cf. Romans 8:38, 39). Those two verses in Romans alone, remembered in the hour of temptation and trial, should suffice to help a counselee get through successfully.

The influence of wicked persons on your counselee is something that you ought always to keep in mind. You may be dealing with a weak counselee who needs to become fortified by appropriate Scripture to stand up to them. Remember I Corinthians 15:33. Notice in that verse, even after one has acquired "good habits," evil companions may corrupt him. Never underestimate the power of evil. It is strong. And there are many who revel in pulling a struggling counselee down into the gutter with them. There is only one thing stronger: the grace of God mediated through His Word (cf. Romans 5:20).

**62 At midnight I will rise to thank You
Because of Your righteous judgments.**

Night is the time when the world is shut out. It is the time of contemplation (cf. v. 55). It is the time of danger. Midnight was in the middle of the night in lands where people went to bed at an early hour and rose with the sun. Yet, because of all that God has so **righteously** done, the Psalmist could not sleep. As he thought about God's mercies to him, he simply had to thank Him for it. When others toss and turn, and miss sleep because of a guilty conscience, because of fear, or whatever, the believer who spends his time thinking about God's goodness will be moved to gratitude.

It may be that the Christian whose nights are fretful ought to be encouraged to think over all the **righteous judgments** of God that have eventuated in blessings to him. Then, rather than fret and worry he may **rise and give thanks**. Keep this in mind the next time that you encounter a counselee who is missing sleep. Don't get him to count sheep; ask him to count his many blessings. The one who **rises to give thanks** will soon lie down in sweet, peaceful sleep! There is altogether too much worry and fear among believers, because there is far too little thanksgiving.

**63 I am a companion of all who fear You,
And of those who keep Your precepts.**

Contrast this verse with verse 61. A true believer chooses the right friends. Proper **companions** encourage proper thinking and proper living. Evil companions do the opposite. When your counselee tells you temptation is great, ask him who among his companions can encourage him in withstanding it. It would be wise for every counselor to collect some of the "one anothering" verses of the Bible to use in discussing such matters. To get you started, take a look at Hebrews 10:24, 25. If a counselee doesn't have good companions (saved persons is what those **who fear You** is referring to), he needs to cultivate them. None of us can go it alone. There are no Lone Ranger Christians. We need each other. That is what the church of Christ can do for him. He should cultivate relationships with other believers. He may begin by chatting with them after services at church. He may invite them to his home. He may ask them to do things with him. Friendships develop when people do things together. If he can become involved in some work in his church he may develop fruitful relationships with others who are also involved in that work. In short, it is every bit as important for this brother or sister to have proper relationships with **those who keep** God's commandments as it is for him to see you. Your counsel can last only so long; a friendship is ongoing and may last for life.

But in encouraging a counselee to develop proper friendships, don't let him think only about the benefit he will receive. The one another passages speak of *mutual* benefits. He also should strive to bring something to the friendship that will encourage others in doing God's will. One of the things he could do is to engage in Bible study with another, or with other believers. The word translated **companion**, literally is "fellow." It is a word that speaks of *fellow*ship with others (cf. our expression "fellow traveler").

**64 Yahweh, Your lovingkindness fills the earth;
Teach me Your statutes.**

Proofs of God's goodness are everywhere. The problem is that "Christless eyes" do not see them. Even Christians see far too little. That is because they don't think rightly; they don't look for evidence of God's mercy. That rain falls on the evil as well as the good alike, leading to fruitful seasons is one such proof (Acts 14:17; Deuteronomy 4:19[b]). That God doesn't eliminate every wicked person when he commits sin is a mercy to him, giving him space for repentance. On and on, one could go, listing the **lovingkindnesses** of God. It is an activity that one also may engage in at night (cf. v. 62). Christians who learn to see God's hand of goodness and mercy all around them every day and hour are rarely those who get depressed, rarely those who complain, rarely those who are a sucker for some false belief, and so on.

The last line is significant. It tells you what to say

when the counselee tells you, "Well, I just have a hard time seeing such things." Your reply? "Ask God to **teach you His statutes** so that by means of them you may be able to have your eyes opened.

TETH

**65 You have been good to Your servant,
Yahweh, according to Your Word.**

With God there should be no surprises. He does exactly as He says He will: He does **good to** His **servants,** *according to His Word.* He said he would, and He does. This, and the rest of the testimonies in this Psalm to the goodness and faithfulness of God ought to impress counselees. If they can't give the same witness to their God—that He does as He said He would in the Bible—one of at least two things is wrong. Either the counselee hasn't the eyes to see, or he isn't eligible for that goodness (i.e., he isn't a genuine **servant** of God). There will be more about God's goodness in this section, and it is all connected to the Bible.

**66 Teach me good discretion and knowledge
Because I have believed Your
commandments.**

Here is a prayer that the Psalmist might know what and how to do what God's commands. That, of course, is needed by all of us. How often is it that a counselee has had the right idea in mind but destroyed his effort because he lacked **good discretion** (taste, judgment, discernment). Here the writer asks for both aspects of what it takes to serve God well. Not only must he know God's will, but *how to* bring it off.

Psalm 119:66

Look carefully at the verse. The writer has believed that what God commands is correct. Intellectually, he is on the right side. He now understands that he needs two things more. He needs to know the specific commands that will guide him in his daily decision-making and he needs to know exactly how to obey them.

Sometimes one who believes that God's Word has the answers fails to ascertain precisely which commands apply to his situation. Or, having found the command, he fails to interpret it properly. Or, having interpreted it properly, he fails to apply it correctly. That is the one side: **good knowledge**. The other side is this: "Now that I know these things, I need a right attitude, proper timing, the correct words, the best context in which to do what I know what God wants me to do." We are not talking about **delay** in order not to obey (cf. v. 60). But we are talking about a counselee who knows what he should do and is anxious to do it—but he may be overanxious. He may lack the sound **discretion** necessary to do it well. By his stumbling, bumbling approach, *intending* to do good, he may do more *harm* than good.

Let's look at a case. Here is one who knows he must confess his wrongdoing to another. You ask him to tell you just what he will say when he does so. "Sure," he replies. Then he proceeds. "I'll tell him that I am sorry I said what I did when he pulled that dirty trick on me." "No, no," you explain. "That's not the way to do it. If you were wrong, talk about the wrong that *you* did. Forget his offense against you at this point; focus on yourself. There will be time enough later to deal with his wrong. If you combine the two, it won't sound like a confession at all, It'll sound as if you were justifying your action. Now let's role play it again. . . ."

The verse, then, is dealing with the more elusive

Psalm 119:68

aspect of obedience: *how one obeys.* As a counselor you cannot be less concerned about the *how-to* than about the *what-to.* Remember that, or you will find counselees discouraged over trying to do the right thing, but failing.

**67 Before I was afflicted I went astray,
But now I have kept Your Word.**

Here is a verse that sings the praises of **affliction**! It is not often that you hear counselees join in the chorus. But it is a song that every counselor must teach his counselees to sing. **Affliction** may come in order to purify. It may be sent in order to turn one back to the proper pathway. When **we go astray** (and we all do from time to time) we often need affliction to wake us up to what we have done and where we have gone. Affliction is to the erring Christian as an alarm clock is to one who is apt to oversleep. Moreover, in addition to awakening us to our sinful ways, it often stops us and provides time for thought. When one is engaged in the hustle-bustle of life, he may take little time to think about his life. When he is stopped in his tracks by the loss of a job, by the onset of a debilitating illness, and the like, it can be a blessing to give him time to think seriously about his ways. There are many ways in which afflictions of all sorts may become a blessing by returning a counselee to the **Word.** This is, therefore, a key verse in the Psalm for every counselor. He should remember it and use it often. It is the answer to much of the whining that he hears. "What have you learned from God's Word during this time of trouble?" is a first class question for you to ask of those who complain.

**68 You are good and do good.
Teach me Your statutes.**

In the wake of the previous verse, the Psalmist probably was thinking of the counterpart of the argument that affliction may be a blessing. Many counselees wonder about God's goodness when affliction comes their way. They say such things as "How could God let this happen to one of His children?" The answer of the biblical counselor always is, "For some **good** purpose." It is true that we may not be able to discern God's purposes at the moment, especially when our noses are pressed tightly against problems. We may need to get some perspective to do so—perhaps even the perspective that comes from being in heaven itself. But if we **believe** God's Word to be true (see the previous verse) then we must believe also that He is **good**, and **does good** to His own. Here is a matter of faith. Stress that while backing up your statement about God's good purpose with this verse. It is a very important verse to use often, as I said, in combination with the previous one.

69 Proud persons have patched together a lie against me;
I will keep Your commandments with my whole heart.

The word translated **patched together** pictures people manufacturing a lie by patching together bits and pieces of supposed facts in order to support it. It shows willful intent to misrepresent the facts, which are often twisted and considered in part in order to do such a thing. These are the sorts of people who are also mentioned in verse 51. They scorn and slander another and must be able to back up their charges. The "backing" they offer, however, is not honest; it is strictly of their own making.

But the important thing is not the **proud** or their activities. The crucial point of the verse is how the Psalmist reacts. Does he fight? Does he argue? Does he complain? Does he retaliate? What he does is to **wholeheartedly** walk according to God's **commandments**. In other words, he is all the more cautious about his lifestyle. He all the more conforms to God's Word.

Counselees react in two ways to lies and slander about themselves; in doing so, either they disobey or obey God. The writer does the latter. So should your counselee. But, chances are, he has done the former; that may be why he is in counseling! Point out the two responses. Make sure that he meets **lies** and slander in the proper way: by turning to the Bible, discovering there what God wants him to do in response and then carefully ordering his response according to Scripture. Not too many counselees do that. Usually, it must be taught, often *argued* from the Bible.

> 70 **Their heart is without feeling, like fat;**
>   **But I delight in Your law.**

Plainly, for the most part, section TETH deals with oppression and other sorts of affliction and how to respond to it. It is therefore a very valuable part of the Psalm for counselors. The idea of **fat** needs some explanation. Unlike our society, biblical writers used the word fat to describe something good. It is often used, for instance, to describe *prosperity*—as it probably does here. These are prosperous persons who, because they live in luxury where every desire is gratified, have lost all **feeling** for those who don't. It may be speaking of the same proud persons mentioned in the previous verses. At any rate, here we meet those who care little for others and their plight.

Obviously, the verse may first apply to the counselor. It is very important for him to be able to be sensitive to the needs and difficulties encountered by his counselees.

Psalm 119:71

It is possible to become insensitive to such matters, to become mechanical in one's approach to counselees. That is the beginning of the end of a counseling ministry. The counselor must "weep with those who weep" as well as "rejoice with those who rejoice." There is no doubt about the need.

But it also applies to the counselee. When oppressed by others who are insensitive to his plight, a counselee should not spend much time moaning and groaning about that. Rather, it should drive him to the Bible, in which he will discover a sensitive Savior who *does* care. Here, he will find the **delights** that he has been denied by others. He may not have the prosperity of the one who has become utterly insensitive, but surely, he may prosper in God's way—spiritually. That is the true wealth anyway!

**71 It is good that I was afflicted
That I might learn Your statutes.**

This verse ought to be considered together with verse 67. Here is the bald statement that when God's providence calls for **affliction** it is **good**. How is that? Well, it seems plain: it brought the writer closer to an understanding of the Bible. He **learned** things from the Scriptures that he would not have learned otherwise. Affliction provided time to study the Bible. It provided impetus to do so. It gave direction to that study. He knew what it was he needed to find in the Bible (his study of the Bible was not unfocused). All of this, and much more, affliction may do. However, sometimes the affliction is not necessary if the Bible study and observance is forthcoming on one's own. But, if one **goes astray** (v. 67), it may take affliction to bring him back to the biblical path. But even God's choicest servants have undergone affliction; sometimes not

Psalm 119:73

because they went astray, but simply to bring them into a closer relationship to their Lord.

**72 To me the law of Your mouth is better
Than thousands of gold and silver.**

When a counselee can honestly say this with the Psalmist, he probably is ready to leave counseling (or nearly so). In II Timothy 3:15 we read that the Scriptures are "God-breathed." This verse reiterates the thought. The biblical writers always equated what is written in the Bible with what is spoken by God. There is never any lesser thought about the written Scriptures being less than God's holy, inspired, inerrant Word.

Because he considers the Bible to be the very word of God written, he places its value far above the most precious metals. It is more valuable to him than riches untold. That is the viewpoint mentioned above when contrasting the insensitive person who prospers in this world with the one who delights in God's law (v. 70). When one comes to this realization and acts on it, he has reached the end of counseling.

YOD

**73 Your hands have made me and formed me;
Give me discernment that I may learn Your commandments.**

The Psalmist not only acknowledges that God is His Creator, but he bases his appeal upon the fact. In essence he says, You **made** me; now make me what I ought to be. He is not blaming God for having done a poor job of making him. No, if you asked him, he would say the opposite.

Psalm 119:73

Rather, the idea seems to be, if **You made me and formed me** into what I became, surely you can *remake* me to overcome the effects of sin that have ruined Your creation. He wants to be able to understand the Bible so that he can carry out the purpose for his existence.

The word for **discernment** is the one used previously. I mentioned at that point that it comes from a word that implies ability to distinguish between things that differ. A great amount of one's study, application and implementation of Scripture involves knowing how to separate look-alikes from those things that truly are alike. For instance, in Romans 12 there is a command to take no vengeance. In Romans 13, God speaks of the ruler as an avenger He sends. How can these two be squared? Simply by the use of such discernment: in chapter 12 you have personal, individual ethics in view. In chapter 13, it is the institution of the state that is in view. The same person acting in personal interests may not take vengeance, yet must do so if acting as an official of the state.

That, and many other such distinctions of various sorts, are essential to the proper use of Scripture in counseling. It is essential, then, for a counselor to know how to use discernment in applying the Bible to the situations in which counselees find themselves. Without it, he will do much harm. So, the plea for discernment ought, first of all, be that of the counselor.

Counselees also need to pray for discernment. They will need it not only in the present situation but in days to come if they are to avoid further complications in their lives. Help them to see the importance of asking God for this. Remember to show them that the answer will come through having their senses "trained" to discern between good and evil by the faithful, earnest study and practice of the Biblical commands (Hebrews 5:11-14).

Psalm 119:74

**74 Those who fear You will rejoice when they
see me
Because I have hoped in Your Word.**

Those about whom the Psalmist speaks are other believers (**those who fear You**). They will **rejoice** when they **see** him because he **has hoped in** God's **Word**. Why should they rejoice? Why should hoping in God's Word lead to this? For at least two reasons. First, all believers ought to **rejoice** when they see others trusting God's Word enough to live according to it. If they don't, there is something radically wrong. All Christians should have a deep concern for the spiritual welfare of other Christians so that when they see growth in them they should automatically be happy about it. Second, those who **fear** God should **rejoice** at meeting other faithful Christians. When moving from one location to another, the Christian, alone among those who live on this earth, discovers (to his delight) that he has "family" everywhere. In our rootless society, others have great difficulty breaking into a new community. Christians who attend a Bible-believing church immediately find fellowship with others who **rejoice** at their arrival. Of course, I am presupposing that the congregation that is attended resembles the kind of church it ought to be. Counselors, make every effort to see that each counselee attends and becomes a part of such a congregation. We all need one another. That is one reason God has developed the fellowship of the saints that Christ called His church. Many believers lack the joy of true fellowship with others who fear God. Check out the possibility that this may be a major problem in any given case.

Psalm 119:75

75 Yahweh, I know that Your judgments are righteous,
And that it is in faithfulness that You have afflicted me.

Consider this verse together with verses 67 and 71. There can be no question about the Psalmist's assertion: he **knows** it to be true. Such certainty in affliction not only is commendable, but is essential to weathering it successfully. Only at this point does it become clear that, though He may use human instrumentality, ultimately the affliction **comes from God**. Some counselees struggle with that fact. But it is your task to show them that is not a problem; it is the solution to one. There is no impersonal, chance that for no good reason has brought **affliction** into his life. If that were so, the universe would be out of control and would have little or no meaning. Prayer would be ridiculous! No, prayer is meaningful because God is sovereign. He is the One Who is engineering all that happens—including affliction—for the good of the counselee (It is in His **faithfulness** that He has done so).

There is nothing unrighteous about what God demands and decrees. The Psalmist declares **Your judgments are righteous**. That is to say they are always the right ones, the holy ones, the fair ones. Counselees may protest to the contrary, but all you need do is to observe that they disagree with the Bible in doing so. Their controversy is not with you; it is with God. He is faithful (cf. I Corinthians 10:13).

How can one say that afflictions from God are given in **faithfulness**? The verses concerning afflictions, mentioned previously, set forth some of the facts that support the contention. In each case these, or other factors, may be pointed out. But in all those cases, one thing is paramount: afflictions are given by God to draw Christians more closely to Himself by bringing them more closely to the Bible. Always make that point in discussing such matters. If the counselee fails to respond to this approach, then ask him, "Why is it that you haven't been drawn more closely to God's Word through this affliction?"

76 I ask that You will let Your lovingkindness comfort me,
Your servant, according to Your Word.

Here the Psalmist begs for God's grace in times of affliction to **comfort** him. How will God answer this request? Will He send certain sensations into his body? Will He speak to him in a dream? Will He give him reassuring signs? How will He do so? He will do it **according to His Word**. That **comfort** will be found in the Bible alone.

And he is concerned to hold God to His Word about that comfort. He wants Him to comfort him as He says that He will in the Bible. In other words, everything that a suffering servant of God does in times of need for comfort will revolve around the Bible. That is what the Psalmist says and believes. That is what should be true in the life of your counselee—and, of course, in the counseling that he receives.

Every counselor should have a number of verses dealing with **comfort**, and how to obtain it, ready at hand. Why not take out your concordance, look up the word (and kindred terms), check out the verses, and list those you think you could use most effectively in some convenient place? Your task is to comfort through the Bible. If you don't know how to it is time you learned.

Psalm 119:77

**77 Let Your lovingkindnesses come to me so
   that I may live,
   Since Your law is my delight.**

When the grace of God (**lovingkindness**) is needed, those who have found many **delights** (the word here is plural, but difficult to translate that way) in God's **law** will be able to ask Him for it on that very basis. If they have been **delighting** in the Bible—learning what God says and reveling in doing it—then when they come into a time of near death they may request the **lovingkindnesses** of God to rescue them from the jaws of death *as they have discovered in God's law that He is delighted to do.* Counselees in dire straits need to understand this and need to do exactly as the Psalmist did. But if they are not delighting in His Word, they need to turn to Him in repentance (as that Word directs) and then begin to do so—even in the midst of serious afflictions (see verses on affliction in this and the previous section).

**78 Let proud persons be ashamed since by lies
   they perverted matters;
   I will meditate on Your precepts.**

Even this didn't divert the Psalmist from spending time **meditating** on God's **precepts**. Indeed, it became a stimulus to do so. Proud, wicked persons who **pervert** facts must and (in God's time) will be brought down in **shame**. If ever there was a time when people get their way by **perverting** the truth, this is it. That means that your counselees will frequently be subject to such treatment (He may also be involved in doing it). They too should ask God to bring the truth to light, thus shaming those who have lied. But in the meanwhile, and it may be quite a while, they are not left without resources. Regardless of what happens, irrespective of what others think, the counselee always may turn to divine precepts to comfort, encourage and direct him in the interim. But this must be no careless, shallow thing; he is to **meditate** on those precepts. And that includes all that was said to be true of genuine biblical meditation in verse 15.

79 Let those who fear You and know Your testimonies return to me.

It seems that believers had abandoned the Psalmist—probably in his affliction. He is calling them to support him in time of need. True friendship is discovered at such times. When others abandon one, those who are genuinely friends will stick to him—even if he needs reproving. The Scriptures teach that a friend sticks closer than a brother (Proverbs 18:24). There is a kinship among those who understand and are committed to God's Word. His **testimonies** are the ground for a solid relationship between believers. It transcends doctrinal differences of a minor sort, going beyond the warts that appear on the faces of all of us. God uses His Word to bind believers together. It is, therefore, particularly hurtful when those who adhere to the Bible find that those they thought were their close friends in the common cause of the Scriptures have left them. It is altogether proper to call them to **return**. On what grounds? On the grounds that they too have known God's **testimonies**.

80 Let my heart be complete in Your statutes So that I may not be ashamed.

The word **complete** (*tam*) has been discussed earlier (cf. v. 1). Here, the Psalmist is doing what James advised. He said that if one was not **complete** (*teleios*) he should ask of God Who answers liberally and without chiding

Psalm 119:81

(James 1). Many counselees realize that they lack something in their lives. That is why they come. It may be that they lack the wisdom to handle various problems they must face. This is because they do not know the **statutes** of God. The Psalmist wants to lack nothing, to be entire (as James put it). He wants all of what God has for him in His Word. He wants to know the entire corpus of God's statutes so that he may grow in every area of his life into the kind of person God wants him to become. That is a good summary statement of all the rest that has been said in this section. One needs to be able to handle prosperity and want. He must know what to do in affliction or ease. He must know God's will about his business, family, social life and every other area as well. That is the prayer of the Psalmist, which ought to become the prayer of all counselors and counselees.

CAPH

**81 My soul perishes for Your salvation;
I hope in Your Word.**

The only thing that sustains the Psalmist in this time of great trial and heartache is God's **Word**. No Christian can meet life's trials apart from it. There is no way in which he can go on without the promises of the Bible as his **hope**. That, of course, is the message to your counselee from this verse. Remember, the word **hope** in the Bible means confident expectation, nothing less. The word translated **perishes** literally means "done in" so as to be weak, powerless, spent. It also means **perishing**. Here when he says that he is longing for (waiting for) God's **salvation**, he does not mean the salvation of his soul (even though at first that is what it seems he is saying). The expression **my soul** in the Psalms almost always (if not always) means simply "me." It is a poetic way of referring to one's self. He is talking about physical salvation. He was already saved spiritually, or he could not have said, **I hope in Your Word**. While awaiting the fulfillments of God's promises regarding his rescue from trouble, he clings to the Bible. That is all that sustains him in this trial. But for the hope found in its pages, he would **perish**. He was, literally, "done in."

**82 My eyes fail for Your Word
While saying "When will You comfort me?"**

As you notice, this verse seems to be related to the first verse in this section. Indeed, unlike others, this section seems to be of a whole. He is near perishing, and his **eyes** are even **failing**. He has strained them to the point of fatigue looking for the help that he has requested. But it has not come. He longs for the fulfillment of the biblical promises that he has claimed. Even in these extremities he will not abandon the Word. The entire section teaches that no matter how bad things may get, one must continue to trust the Scriptures. He continues:

**83 I have become like a wineskin bottle in the
  smoke;
Yet I do not forget Your statutes.**

No matter how difficult a time may get, there is never reason to **forget** God's **statutes**. The picture here is of a wineskin heated over a fire until it becomes dried out and begins to crack. He had become dried, brittle, shriveled up. Yet he continued to trust God's Word. Once more the same message is conveyed, but even more vividly.

The tendency when one is tested by the fires of adversity is to complain, give up or respond in some simi-

Psalm 119:84

lar way. Indeed, a person can become nearly impossible to live with under such conditions. Not the Psalmist: he was suffering greatly, but he still trusted in God's promises. Suffering ought not make a true Christian cynical so as to forget God's statutes; rather, it ought to bring him even closer to them.

**84 How many are the days of Your servant?
When will You judge my persecutors?**

The two questions are those that constantly came to mind during this period of suffering. The first is, "How much longer can I take this adversity and live?" I guess the answer to it is simply this: "Not many more days unless it is lifted." There are two ways in which God rescues His own from affliction. One is by removing the affliction; the other is by removing the person from the affliction. In the latter case, that (again) happens in two ways. God may cause him to be removed physically from the circumstances or He may take him to be with Himself. It seems that the last alternative was in the mind of the writer when he asked this question.

The second question, **When will You judge my persecutors?** reminds one of the martyrs' call for judgment in the Book of Revelation (Revelation 6:10). It is not wrong for a believer to ask this question of God. The **judgment** mentioned in the verse is the one to which the Word sentences all such. It is for God to fulfill His promises to him in adversity and toward them in judgment that the Psalmist calls.

**85 The proud have dug pits for me,
Something that is not according to Your law.**

He now continues, stating why the persecutors (the **proud**) deserve judgment. Totally disregarding God's

Word (cf. Exodus 21:34) they **dug pits** for the express purpose of having the Psalmist fall into them. They want to trap him as they would trap a wild beast. Whether this is to be taken literally or not is irrelevant. Either way, they went to extremes to do harm to him. Clearly, what they did was contrary to the Bible. That is the ground upon which he asks for their **judgment**. It is a just and biblical ground.

86 All Your commandments are reliable.
 They persecute me with lying; help me!

Here is a cry for help. The lies have become so severe that they too have become a means of persecuting him. Beaten down from all sides, the persecution seemingly interminable, the Psalmist still holds on to God's Word, which he declares is **reliable** (literally, "faithful"). Persecution, as it is described in this section might have led another to deny the reliability of God's Word. But, like Job, he will not relinquish his trust. Indeed, it is precisely because he held to God's reliable Word that he was able to hold on under persecution when others might have given up. That is the message for counselees.

87 They had almost done me in on earth,
 But I did not forsake Your precepts.

More dependence on God's Word is evident. The verse is saying in other words what he has been saying all along.

88 According to Your lovingkindness give me
  life
 And I will keep the testimonies of Your
  mouth.

Once more, notice that the writer considers the writ-

Psalm 119:89

ten Word identical with the spoken Word of God. That is contrary to all neo-orthodox teaching. The verse is not some foxhole promise. ("Save me and I will obey You.") No, exactly not. He has held on to the **testimonies** of God through thick and thin. He is saying, "If I am rescued from this persecution I will not change; I will continue to keep them. Indeed, if You save me, I will be able to honor You before men by doing so." He is desirous of being saved *in order to* show God's way to others by **keeping** His commandments.

This section, as I noted above, is a whole. Perhaps I should have shown the connections more clearly. But when using it with counselees, don't fail to use all of the verses. One of its principal benefits to counselees is to show that their situation is not unique. Other saints have suffered immeasurably before them. Yet, these saints were able to remain true to God and continue to depend on His Word through it all. That means they can do so too—if they will.

LAMDEH

**89 Forever, Yahweh,
Your Word is settled in heaven.**

Man may do what he can to deny, destroy or otherwise pervert God's **Word** on earth. That changes nothing; it is **settled in heaven**. It is beyond sinful man's longest reach. It is **settled**; that is, it is sure, certain, unchangeable, fixed. God's Word is unlike man's, which has all of the opposite characteristics. Because that is so, God is reliable. It is something that you can depend upon. That is something that no other counselor can say of his counsel.

Psalm 119:90

That is something no other counselee has. It is unique among the various counseling methods. No one else has an absolutely unchangeable, dependable source of true counseling data. One wonders, then, why Christians become enamored with anything else. In light of this verse to do so is absurd.

This verse is speaking about absolutes. Worldly counselors abhor absolutes. They want to be able to change things from time to time; to move along with the fads. They prefer to revise their methods according to their own likes and dislikes. They do not want to be "tied down" to facts and principles and methods that are fixed. That is because they are in rebellion against God. They do not want to do things His way (cf. Isaiah 55:8),

Yet, it is precisely the absolute nature of the Bible that makes it effective. There is no other standard that could be universal; it is the only one. It is such because only man's Creator has the right to impose a universal standard. Because each sinner "does that which is right in his own eyes," there is no harmony. It is the one authoritative source of truth and, therefore, it alone could bring peace and harmony. Think, counselor: that is what God has provided you.

You do not have to decide which parts of a system are correct or are in error, which parts you must revise and which you may keep as they are, which parts you must eclectically replace with some other. It is *all* true, fixed, settled—by God—and placed out of your reach. That is not only what makes the Bible unique; it is what makes it so valuable to the counselor.

**90 Your faithfulness is for all generations;
You founded the earth and it stands.**

Like the **standing** earth is God's **faithfulness**. That is

Psalm 119:90

the comparison in the verse. It is reliable. Indeed, it is even more reliable than the present earth is. Some day the earth itself will melt and be remolded. Since God's Word is already perfect, it needs no such reshaping.

And since it is fixed in the heavens (v. 89), and thus is unchangeable, it is available to **all generations**. You don't need to produce something new to correspond to changing times. The One Who knows the end from the beginning gave us His **faithful** (dependable) Word which serves all men in every generation. That is because, at heart, sinners do not change. That which served them in Paul's day or Calvin's serves them equally well today. The Word provided by God is the one absolute in life.

When you have an absolute, it allows you to breath easily. You don't have to ask, for instance, whether you are permitted to commit adultery under certain circumstances, and try to figure out what they may be. No. You are *never* permitted to commit adultery because that word is settled in the heavens (i.e., by God Himself) and it is for every generation—without exception. That fact makes counseling authoritative.

That is not to say that every counselor, or the counsel he offers, is settled, is absolute. He is also limited by his sin. He too is a sinner, though redeemed and used by God if he is faithful. Yet, he is not omnipotent or free from error. He has much to learn as long as he is in this life. His recollection of the proper verses to use in a given counseling case, for example, may be faulty. His interpretation of the infallible, absolute Word of God may be in error, etc. "Well, then," you ask, "how is he any better off than a pagan counselor?" Much in every way! The pagan must begin by asking "To whom should I turn in this generation as my counseling authority?" He must make the decision himself (sinner, errorist that he is). Moreover, he must decide which elements in Freud, Rogers, Maslow, Jung, etc. (if any) are those he will use in counseling and which he will discard or replace. Since nothing is truly authoritative, nothing is fixed in the heavens; he knows that tomorrow, the whole may need to be junked. He knows that he really can know nothing for sure. Only arrogant persons would say otherwise. The biblical counselor starts with something permanent, fixed, true and authoritative from the living God. His problem is very small, by comparison. Moreover, he has the Holy Spirit within to enable him to understand and apply the truths that he discovers in this Book. He is miles and miles ahead of the unsaved counselor (or the Christian counselor who depends on the changeable ideas and systems of sinful men). He has the Word of God, the Creator, to which to turn. That makes all the difference. He doesn't need to change systems with the fads.

**91 They stand this day according to Your
       judgments
       For all Your servants.**

As the writer said in the last verse, the **judgments** of God are for **all generations**. They **stand**, fixed, dependable and available for every one of God's **servants** to enlighten them, to guide them, to rebuke them, to encourage them, to counsel them—in all things necessary for life and godliness.

There are no exceptions. Everything that is in the Bible has a place in the life of every Christian. It is sufficient for life and godliness. There is no surplus that must be rejected and done away with, as in every other counseling approach. And there is no Christian who can rightly say, "Well, I only have to read and understand certain parts of the Bible." No, at some point, for some purpose or other, *all* of it has a vital place in his life—even if he may not see how at the moment. Because he is able to operate reasonably well with those parts of Scripture he knows, he doesn't realize that the other parts would make his life more acceptable to Jesus Christ. In principle, everything in Scripture applies to every Christian, regardless of who he is. That is one reason counselors must ever continue to study the Bible.

**92 Unless Your law had been my delight,
Long ago I would have perished in my affliction.**

(Cf. vv. 50, 71.) He had nothing more to depend upon. All else was stripped away by **affliction**. But the Bible was sufficient to help him—even in that sort of extremity. And when your counselee comes claiming the same thing (correctly or not) you may remind him of this verse. If there is nothing else, there is always the Word of God settled, fixed, certain. That is enough to **delight** the one who has nothing else. It may make him appreciate the Word for what it is for the first time. When a counselee develops that sort of mentality, it will make all the difference in him. Work toward it with all you have. Those who **delight** in God's law can find their way out of (or through) any trouble this world has to offer; of that they may be certain. That is what he is about to say in the next verse: he was about to perish, but by depending upon and following God's law, he was snatched from the jaws of death.

**93 I will never forget Your precepts;
By them You have given me life.**

Too many counselees are in counseling because they have *forgotten* God's **precepts**. To forget them and to depend on one's own ideas (or the ideas of others) to make decisions in life is to head for trouble. Once God has rescued one from some extreme situation by His law, he will not easily **forget** its power and effectiveness. Perhaps that is one reason many counselees have little appreciation for the Scriptures, why They play so small a part in their lives. If you can help them out of some serious problem by means of the Bible, you may be able to change their whole perspective on the Word. It is essential, therefore, that from beginning to end you make it clear in counseling that it is not your wisdom, nor some special ability that *you* have that is going to make any difference in their lives, but solely the Holy Spirit blessing the use of His Word, the Bible.

94 I am Yours;
Save me since I have sought Your precepts.

The writer pleads with God to **save** him from some adversity on a twofold basis: he belongs to God; he has **sought** to learn and do God's will as it is recorded in God's Word. That is always a good plea. It is one that honors God and one that brings results.

He is God's. If something should happen to him contrary to the Bible's promises, that would dishonor God. That is why he can effectively ask his heavenly Father to **save** him from such an untoward circumstance. God will not break His promises. Moreover, he has **sought** to learn God's will and to do it. That is pleasing to God. As a **servant** of God he will always be on display as serving Him. Back in the days of Renaissance England, servants wore the livery (uniform) of their lord. What they did reflected on the lord they served because everyone knew whose livery they wore. If a person stole something at the town market and ran with it, everyone knew exactly where to

Psalm 119:95

go to find it. The livery gave him away. The same is true of an up-front Christian who makes it known that he serves Jesus Christ. Everyone knows it. When he is in trouble, therefore, everyone is watching to see if the God Whom he claims has promised to save him from it will do so. When he does something well, he brings honor to God.

95 The wicked have waited for me to destroy me;
I will consider Your testimonies.

"You discover that people are going to lengths to **destroy** you; what is your next move?" That is a good question to ask of a counselee when you want to point him to the Bible. It is especially good if, when you turn to Scripture to **consider** a passage in depth, he becomes impatient with you for doing so. If he says something other than "I will turn to the Bible," or words to that effect (as he is likely to), you may read this verse to him and show him what God expects him to do in trouble.

Point out also that you are not talking about taking some quick glance at a passage that then is applied apart from the understanding and proper thought that God commends. No. What He applauds by means of placing this verse in His holy Word is due **consideration** of the Bible. That alone is what He commends. That is to say, it is not a waste of time to sit down with the Bible (and even some Bible helps—commentaries, Bible dictionaries, etc.) at such a time to work hard at finding out God's will in the circumstance.

Instead, many want a hurry-up solution to their problems, thereby getting themselves even deeper into some mess. They settle for "signs" that God has not authorized, or for "promptings," or for "feelings, sensings" that the

Psalm 119:96

Bible neither recommends nor countenances. All of these things are man—initiated attempts to discover God's will. God is by no means obligated to respond to these attempts. And there is no reason to expect Him to do so, when the answer to one's questions is already inscribed in Scripture. The Bible is not a man-initiated effort to discover God's will. Rather, it is a God-initiated revelation of it (cf. II Peter 1:21). When men ignore what God has given and turn instead to some man-made idea of how to discover God's will, they can expect more trouble than solutions. It is important, then, to make this fact clear. This is an excellent verse from which to make the point. For more on this problem, see my book on biblical guidance, *The Christian's Guide to Guidance*.

**96 I have seen an end to all perfection;
Your commandment is exceedingly broad.**

This is a powerful verse to carry about with you in readiness when counseling. People claim that ways other than God's are freer, fuller, better. They are wrong—and this verse tells them so! What does it mean? Just this: There are claims of **perfection** everywhere, but no matter how good they may seem, they all have their limits. They are all flawed somewhere. They all are narrow, confining; the Bible alone brings liberty and freedom (cf. v. 45). The **end** of everything else is readily apparent to the thinking Christian. He sees that it is not perfect, not sufficient, lacks much. There are limits to what *can* be known, what *is* known. There are limits to ability, power, authority. Nothing apart from God is limitless. No knowledge is as vast as that which He has deigned to give to us.

But God's commandments are all **exceedingly broad**. That is, they are far beyond our fathoming them *in toto* in this world. They are not narrow, confining in

Psalm 119:97

scope. They cover all of life in principle. They are never outdated. On and on one may go, striking out in all directions, and still not reach the limits. That is the point. The Bible may be studied throughout one's life and he may still learn more each time. That is one reason why Biblical counselors keep studying; they can always learn more.

When counselees complain that God is restricting them, read this verse. They need to be shown the vast possibilities for help and learning that God has made available to them.

MEM

**97 How I love Your law!
All day it is my meditation.**

The word for **meditation** in this verse is "musing" (cf. Psalm 1:2). While one is engaged in this sort of meditation, it is true that he may be uttering some sort of prayers as well (that is, presumably, why some translations have "prayer"). The verb **love** is in the preterite, referring to what has been and still is the writer's practice.

Here is the ideal for the counselee: to come to the place where he so **loves** the **law** of God that **all day** he thinks about it in relationship to whatever it is that he must do at any given time. He is not speaking of some occupation with Scripture that so consumes him that he fails to assume his responsibilities. No, precisely not that. Rather, it is a *use* of the Bible in confronting life's happenings that is in view. All day long he is biblically guided in his speech, his thoughts, his deeds. That is the idea.

When one is thus using the Word of God produc-

Psalm 119:98

tively, he will soon come to **love** it. He will see how **broad** and how practical its applications are to daily life. And in turn, as he learns to **love** it, he will meditate on it all the more in this way. This is the opposite of a vicious circle; rather, it is a victorious circle! Explain these facts to the counselee and set him on this pathway.

> **98 By Your commandments You make me
> wiser than my enemies
> Since they are ever with me.**

God's **commandments**, meditated upon all day (being **ever with** one, as explained in the last verse) clearly make any Christian superior in wisdom to his enemies. He has something that they do not possess: the guidance of the living God! How can they begin to match that? They can't.

If it turns out that a counselee's enemies are **wiser** than he, that can only be because he either does not know enough of God's Word or, knowing, has failed to use it on those occasions in which he might have thought, acted or spoken more **wisely**. It is essential, then, to help counselees to learn the Bible and how to use it day-by-day as they live at home, at work and elsewhere. If they do not know how to do so, you might set them to work using the book, *What to do on Thursday*, which is a handbook containing a method for learning how to use the Bible in dealing with problems every day in the week. It details one way to learn to move from the problem to the Bible for answers and then to go back to the problem and deal with it God's way.

You see, according to the last part of the verse, what it is that makes the writer **wiser** than his enemies: he has the Bible **ever with** him. Like a trusted sword, the Sword of the Spirit is there for him to fight with those enemies so

Psalm 119:99

as to conquer them God's way (cf. Romans 12:21). If he is not aware of it, your counselee is in a war that God Himself declared (Genesis 3:15). He cannot help but have enemies if he is living for Him. So it is your task to help him become more proficient in wielding the weapon that God has provided. See my book, *Christian Living in the World*.

**99 I have more understanding than all my teachers
Since Your testimonies are my meditation.**

There is no question about the fact that the Bible gives one better instruction than any human teacher can. The best thing, therefore, for a counselor to do is to point his counselees to the Scriptures. He must, however, interpret them and show him how to **meditate** on them (see above). It is not enough to merely tear verses out of the Bible like a physician ripping a prescription from his pad, saying "take these three times a day with prayer." While God can use even this poor method—because He is not limited by us, and because He works through His Word—it is not what He wants you to do.

In the Bible you are able to discover the proper **understanding** of life. You are able to learn what all of the philosophers of all time did not. You have in your possession the very words of God. They are infallibly true, inerrant and absolute. What a treasure! That is the sort of instruction that no mere teacher can impart.

**100 I understand more than the aged
Because I keep Your precepts.**

Of course, he is speaking of his elders who do not **keep** God's word. If his elders are also faithful in doing so, their long experience in the use of Scripture can be a

Psalm 119:101

great help to him. But, here, like his enemies, the teachers and the aged persons in view are those who do not have the advantage of turning to God in life's decision-making.

Often counselors are young. They must not allow counselees to "despise their youth" (I Timothy 4:12). Remember, they are there because they have not been able to resolve some issue in spite of their age. Age alone does not mean wisdom. Many older persons have done wrong things for so long that they are etched into their lifestyles. You will discover that they have much work to do to replace these patterns with their biblical alternatives. You are there to help them. If they ask why you think that your way is so superior to theirs, then turn to this verse. But you'd better be ready to back up the advice you gave with biblical evidence for why it is. Of course, you ought to be able to show from the Scriptures exactly why you advise anything to anyone at any time anyway.

**101 I have withheld my feet from every evil way
So that I might keep Your Word.**

The path of temptation leads to sin. Counselees must be advised to keep off it. One does not walk as near to the edge of the mountain pass as he can, but stands back from it to preclude the possibility of falling. "Let him who thinks that he stands take heed lest he fall" (I Corinthians 10:12).

In this verse, there is a see saw. If ones **feet** are on the wrong path, they cannot be on the right one; conversely, if they are on the right one, they will not be on the wrong one. It is a matter of choosing the way that one will go. Make it clear to counselees who want to keep a foot on each path that they will diverge so greatly he cannot do so. He will end up on the path of sin. He must make a

Psalm 119:102

deliberate choice and effort to place his feet on the right path and stay there!

You will find that there are those who want to have it both ways. They will insist that it is O.K. to do so. What they need to see is that God's way is antithetical to every other. Because of that, it is impossible to choose. That is what they do not want to do—choose. Insist that it is necessary (Joshua 24:15).

**102 I have not turned away from Your judgments
Since You have taught me.**

Why should he do so? If God, Himself, has **taught** him (lit., "pointed the way"), why should he go elsewhere for a second opinion? That is the question. It is important to pose questions in this antithetical form (see the last verse), since many have been trained to think on a relativistic continuum. Because they do not think antithetically (God's way vs. all others) they want to put together bits and pieces from various sources. No eclecticism is possible with God. He will not share His will with the will of men! Think about this. Make it plain to counselees who have been trained to think otherwise. There are many who don't want to see things stacked up against one another that way; they want to find some truth in everything as well as some error. No! God's Word is absolute truth; in it is no error. Man's word, if it isn't exactly the same as God's (i.e., biblically-derived) is wrong. Put it to counselees that way.

God is the real teacher; it is not you or anyone else. If you do not help counselees to see that—that they are faced with God's teaching in the Bible—you have done them a disservice. Never let a counselee leave counseling thinking that he is merely rejecting something that *you* have said if you can help it. Be sure that what you advise is thoroughly biblical, and make it clear that when he **turns away** from it, he is turning from God, Who **teaches** in the Word.

**103 How sweet Your words are to my palate,
Sweeter than honey to my mouth!**

Well, there you have it! When one recognizes that the Bible is what it is, experiences the truth of its teaching in his life and finds himself drawn closer to God through it, he can do little more than exclaim that it is **sweeter** to him **than honey**. Honey was the universal sweetener in that day. He is saying, therefore, that it is the sweetest thing that he knows. He relishes the teachings of the Bible more than sweets. If there isn't at least a little of this in the life of your counselee, he has a long way to go. Ask him, "Which of these words would you use to describe the Bible: bitter, hard, sweet, frothy, other?" The answer might tell you much. To many it is at best bittersweet. That is sad. And it is so because it reproves, rebukes, convicts and points to paths in which the counselee is failing to walk. Your task, counselor, is to so open up the jar of honey for him that he too will soon agree with the writer of this Psalm.

**104 Through Your precepts I get understanding;
Therefore, I hate every false way.**

Do you counselor? If you truly are nurtured on the Bible in your counseling, you will **hate**. You will find yourself unable to refrain from doing so. If there is no hatred in you for falsehood and what it is doing to your counselees, you must examine your thinking. Something is wrong. Possibly, you fail to see the antithetical nature of what biblical counseling is all about (as I have already

Psalm 119:105

mentioned in this section). It is a contest for the hearts and souls of counselees. You are engaged in warfare. There are enemies. There are false ways. And when someone comes into counseling, having been advised by another counselor to do something entirely opposed to God's Word, you ought to **hate** what you hear. Why? Because it is harmful to the counselee. Because it might destroy others as well. But most of all because it is teaching that is opposed to God's teaching.

If you come to an **understanding** of God's precepts, you recognize immediately what is true and what is false. They say that bank tellers are not taught what false money looks like; because they deal with so much real money, they instinctively know when they are handling false bills. Whether that is still true or not, the principle is applicable to truth. Once one comes to **understand** it, he is fully aware of that which is **false**. And he should **hate** it. If *you* don't, that may be the measure of *your* love for God. In Psalm 97:10 you are directed, "You who love the Lord, hate evil." Beginning with evil in yourself, learn to do so.

NUN

**105 Your Word is a lamp to my feet
And a light to my path.**

The Psalmist is speaking of God's Word giving direction by night (**lamp**) and by day (**light**). To throw **light** on where one is walking is to be a guide to enlighten him about the way to go. This is a dark world. In Scripture, the word darkness speaks of ignorance, sin and death— light, the opposite. The world hates the light because it exposes its evil deeds. Christians rejoice in the light (truth)

Psalm 119:106

because it guides them in God's way (cf. II Peter 1:19.)

Most counselees come explicitly to find out what to do, which way to go. They are in the dark; otherwise they would not be there. You are a dealer in light. Therefore, if what you say doesn't enlighten confused counselees, it is useless. You are there to say about each one's condition exactly what God has already said in His enlightening Word. It is no more your task to darken what He has said by refusing to mention the hard things, than to do so by refusing to shine the light on the wonderful truths that delight. You must enlighten by the word, wherever the **lamp** throws its light.

The way to go is found in the Bible. It, and it alone, is the **lamp** by which every Christian must discover God's will. Light may not be obtained by other means. Notice that it is God's Word alone that is called the **lamp**, the **light**. This lamp throws light on the correct road. It also exposes the false ways of the world. It is essential in a dark place to have a source of light. But the more that one uses it, the more it becomes like the noonday sun that enlightens everything (Proverbs 4:18).

**106 I have sworn—and I confirm it—
That I will keep Your righteous judgments.**

Here is commitment. The oath is a serious matter; one does not take an oath lightly. God holds him to it. But the Psalmist, by **confirming** his oath, is holding himself to his oath. From the weaknesses that he is willing to admit in other verses, however, one must suppose that this oath is taken with the understanding that he cannot fulfill it in his own wisdom and strength. It is the Holy Spirit Who alone can enable him to **keep** those **righteous judgments** of God. Every Christian, familiar with grace will understand this matter. Any promises of this sort that he

Psalm 119:107

makes will be conditioned by the idea that the **righteousness** in view is totally from God.

First, righteousness is imputed (counted) to the believer. It is Christ's holy life that is reckoned to his account. Then, going on in his life, he is blessed with an actual righteousness (the righteousness referred to in this verse) that is imparted bit by bit as the Holy Spirit conforms him to the Word of God.

What is remarkable about this verse is the fact that the Psalmist does not simply make an oath, then go away and forget it. He keeps on **confirming** it to God. The counselee is not immune to forgetting his promises to God. He too should be taught to regularly **confirm** those promises. When flying overseas, one must confirm his flight with his airline so many hours before returning. If he doesn't, there is no promise that they will reserve his seat. This confirmation means that he will phone the airline and assure them that, indeed, he plans to take the flight that he booked. In much the same way, in times of difficulty (especially), the counselee will do well to **confirm** his promises to keep whatever commandments of God are in view at the moment. Unlike the example of the airline, the confirmation is mainly for his own benefit. While it is wise for counselors to encourage counselees to do this, there are times when they must ask them if they are still committed to doing God's will (i.e., they must know whether the counselee will **confirm** his commitment).

**107 I am severely afflicted, Yahweh;
Give me life according to Your Word.**

We have seen before how, when at a point of extremity in which life itself is in jeopardy, the Psalmist thinks of God's **Word**. It is in that Word that he finds all he needs.

Psalm 119:108

Everything else and everyone else may fail him in that hour; God's promises, set forth in His **Word** will not.

Help the counselee to think similarly. Tell him in time of need to think about what he has been learning concerning his situation from the Bible. Help him to see that this will bring God before his mind, this will lead him to pray in ways that are based on the promises in Scripture. In a time when one is falling, he grabs whatever is at hand. If the Word of God is not uppermost in his mind at such moments, he will grab for something else. That is why he must meditate on the Word day and night—throughout the whole day. That is why he must store up God's Word in his heart. If he does so faithfully, his normal, habitual response will be to "grab" for the promises of God when he senses he is beginning to fall. That is the response that you ought to work toward in all your counselees.

108 Yahweh, please accept the freewill offerings of my mouth
And teach me Your judgments.

The Psalmist understood the purpose of the temple sacrifices. In themselves, they did nothing for the offerer. They were symbolic of a deeper, nonphysical offering that **Yahweh** expected. Here, he penetrates the meaning of the **freewill offering**—it was an offering of thanksgiving that was not required, but if offered, was so regulated that it expressed the gratitude of the worshipper. Hosea 14:2 plainly shows that this spiritual meaning of the offerings was clear to genuine Old Testament saints. In Hebrews 13:15 the inner meaning of the sacrifices is exposed. The sacrifice is from the **mouth**. That is to say, it was a sacrifice of prayer and praise that he was making to God. He was asking God to **accept** (look favorably

Psalm 119:109

upon) that praise and thanksgiving as He **accepted** Abel's sacrifice, and not to reject it as He did Cain's.

The counselee (knowing that he is a sinner) must also come before God humbly. He prays, not demanding something from God, but in deference to His holiness requests that God will even **accept** his praise. How much more so ought his prayer be in humility when he is requesting something for himself!

Most of all, the fact that he was grateful and desired to show his gratitude in prayer, is apparent in this verse. Too often we cry out to God in our need, then when He meets it according to His riches in glory in Christ Jesus, we forget to give thanks. We are an ungrateful people who live in an age of ingratitude (cf. II Timothy 3:1ff.). Counselors must teach counselees not only to turn to God in their need, but to turn to Him in gratefulness when that need is satisfied. By the ways in which they, themselves, remember to do so during prayer in sessions, the counselor sets the example, and thereby most effectively teaches the counselee.

**109 My soul is in my hand continually,
Yet I do not forget Your law.**

What does this mean? From Judges 12:3, I Samuel 19:5, and other passages, we understand the figure of speech. For someone to carry his **soul** (life) **in his hand** means to have it in a vulnerable place. It is to be in jeopardy **continually**. Though this was so, he did not become so wrapped up in his troubles, so concerned about his life that he forgot everything else. No, exactly not so. Rather, recognizing that he was continually in such a vulnerable position drove him to God's **law**. Like all that we have been saying throughout this exposition of Psalm 119, trouble, risk, sickness, persecution—whatever negative

Psalm 119:110

comes into a counselee's life—ought to make him think all the more of the Bible and its promises. That is the goal of counseling. It is not merely to solve some presentation problem. It is to help the counselee for the days ahead to think differently about trouble, to cause him to turn to the Bible for God's help in hours of crisis. Having established that fact, and developed the means by practice in actual situations week by week, you will have made an important lifetime change for good in a counselee.

Sometimes one runs risks by doing what the Bible tells him to do. In other words, obedience to God is the very reason he **holds his life in his hand**. If that is the case, it is easy to **forget** God's **law** (in the sense of not wishing to do it) in order to remain safe. The martyrs and the confessors of every age have faced that temptation. But the believer who loves God is willing to walk God's paths even though he must do so with his soul in his hand! There is a certain courageous element in what the Psalmist is saying and in what you must encourage the counselee to consider from the bottom of his heart.

110 The wicked have set a trap for me,
Yet I am not wandering from Your precepts.

Daniel continued to pray as he had from the beginning even though it placed his life in danger. The heroic, courageous element mentioned in the exposition of the last verse is set forth even more clearly in this verse. The Psalmist is aware of the designs of the **wicked**. But even though he recognizes their perfidy he does not fail to do as he ought before God. He still walks in God's **precepts**. Those pathways on which he was walking in obedience to God were what brought the wrath of the wicked down upon his head. Yet, he will not **wander** from them. He will not let the threats of wicked men divert him from the way of God.

Psalm 119:111

There is a perverseness about those who refuse to serve and honor God. They want to stamp out any reference to Him—whether it be verbal or whether it be in the lifestyle of a believer. Thus, they are concerned to drive the believer from his course of action. The counselee must be urged to be courageous on such occasions, refusing to turn aside from God's way.

111 I have taken Your testimonies as a heritage forever;
They make my heart rejoice!

Yes. There is no reason ever to abandon God's **testimonies**. They are eternally valid. And the Psalmist, so grateful for them, wants never to have to give them up. As one rejoices in receiving and entering into an **inheritance**, so the Psalmist treats God's testimonies. They are his inheritance. And they are such that, unlike a human inheritance, he will never have to leave them behind for another.

The counselee must be brought to the realization that he too has been left a valuable **heritage**. The prophets and the apostles, under the inspiration of the Holy Spirit, wrote these books of the Bible, containing the very words of God for him and all who would believe in Jesus Christ throughout all time. He should be grateful to them. He should also be grateful to all those throughout history who died to preserve this **heritage** for him—the reformers and other saints, many of whom were burned at the stake for holding fast to the Bible. Most of all, he should be grateful that God originally gave the inheritance. It is a precious gift to him. He ought to recognize it for that and nothing less. Perhaps he has never thought of the Bible this way before. Wouldn't it be good to read this verse to him in order to make it clear how he too ought to view the Scriptures?

**112 I have bowed my heart to do Your statutes—
To the end.**

The **bowing** of the **heart** is a genuine submission to the will of God revealed in the Word of God. It is not some outward submission required and exacted under outside pressure. No. It is genuine because it comes from the Psalmist's **heart**. That is, it comes from within. It is the result of the Holy Spirit's work within him (Romans 5:5).

But notice the new element: **to the end**. He will not give up. He will persevere to the end. How many go astray in old age! It is as though they say, "Well, I've done my part; let someone else take over now." That sentiment may be correct in many other areas, but certainly it must not be carried over to obedience to God's **statutes**. There is a reward at the end to those who persevere to the end.

It is easy to succumb to temptation when one is tired and worn out. Age brings many problems with it. There are the aches and pains, the illnesses, the inability to think and do as in the past. All that is true. But if one has so habituated himself to do God's will in days before, these righteous habits will persist even when the ability to respond grows weaker. It is important to look ahead today and ask, "Will what I am doing now be my strength or my undoing in old age?" That is an important question that far too few consider. Don't deprive your counselees of such thinking.

Psalm 119:113

SAMECH

**113 I hate doubting ways,
But I love Your law.**

So did James (cf. James 1). The word **doubting** is a peculiar one. It comes from the idea of a branch which spreads out in all directions. The picture is of one reaching like that branch here and there seeking help. It is the antithesis of the Christian's approach to problems: he **loves** God's **law**. How are they set over against one another? This way: the unbeliever turns here and there, never satisfied with the answers he gets because they are not true answers at all. The Psalmist, on the other hand, always goes to one place alone—God's **law**. He does this because he always finds a satisfying answer in it. That, then, is why he **loves** it.

Why does he **hate** doubting ways? Because they only confuse, they only let people down. But most of all, because they are opposed to God's certain ways. If a counselee turns here and there like the branch spreading out in all directions he dishonors God. He ought to know where to go, and without doubts rest firmly on the promises and principles of the Bible. In that way he not only finds true answers to his questions, real solutions to his problems, firm directions to go, but He honors God in doing so. That is the principal thing!

**114 You are my hiding place and my shield;
I hope in Your Word.**

The place to find shelter and protection is in God. How does one secure it? By trusting in God's **Word**. To hope in it is to expectantly trust one's self to whatever God says in it. That is explicit faith. One must realize that if he is trusting for and expecting salvation in the gospel which is found in the Bible, then he ought to be able to fully trust God for lesser things. If the greater, then surely the lesser! In contrast to the branch, the Scriptures provide certainty (a great word of Reformation times). Help counselees to see the Bible as a firm, certain base on which to build one's life and expectations.

Not every counselee seems to see things that way. Many are willing to trust God's Word for their eternal salvation, but when it comes to other (far lesser) matters in this life, they balk. That is totally unreasonable. But sin is unreasonable. Therefore, the counselee often must be brought to see how unreasonable his lack of trust and his failure to hope in God's promises is.

There is much in life that endangers. Teach counselees to find their **hiding place** in God and their **shield** in Him as these are presented in the Bible. God protects in His ways, not necessarily in the ways that we would dictate, had we the power to do so. Therefore, it is necessary not merely to come to God in danger, but to come His way, doing what He says, expecting what He promises. One can find these things only in the Bible.

115 Depart from me evildoers!
I will keep my God's commandments.

The two are incompatible. One cannot remain in the presence of evildoers, listening to their suggestions, running with them, and still follow God's **commandments**. Again, the counselee must make a choice. Many people do not like to position the two (evildoers/God's commands) against each other. But the Psalmist, under inspiration, shows us the necessity of doing so. You cannot follow the ways of men like Freud, Rogers and others who despised God and the Scriptures at the same time.

Psalm 119:116

You must choose between them. You cannot go East and West at the same time; you will come apart if you try! When friends, other counselors, psychologists, psychiatrists, or whoever tell a counselee to do what God forbids in the Bible, or when they tell him not to do what God commands, the counselee must tell them to **depart**. There is a time for you, counselor, to tell a counselee that he cannot counsel with diametrically opposed views of two persons at once. He must choose between them. If a person who has been counseling with another comes to find out what I have to say, I usually tell him, "I'll meet with you once and explain what we are going to do. Then you must dismiss the other counselor, if you want to continue to meet with me. If you try to burn the candle at both ends you will only be burned yourself."

Always check to see if there is someone who is influencing your counselee to do things displeasing to God. If you discover that there is, tell him to sever the relationship—at least until he becomes strong enough to influence that person for good. In all relationships influence takes place. Either the counselee is influencing another for good, or the evildoer is influencing him for evil. There can be no relationships in which influence is not present.

**116 Uphold me by Your Word that I may live,
And let me not be ashamed of my hope.**

Here is a prayer that the Psalmist may **live** (escape life-threatening danger) in order that by being saved from the danger he may honor God before others. If God's promises should fail, He would be dishonored (that is what is meant by his being **ashamed**).

But how would he be able to endure persecution and affliction from his enemies? How would he come through without his expectations failing? How would he be able to

Psalm 119:118

honor God? The **Word** of God would **uphold** him through it all. It supports, it encourages, it promises, it points the way through and out of the danger. The Bible was given by God for just such purposes. That is wonderful to know. But counselees who fail to avail themselves of the Word will be **ashamed**. Their **hope** is not grounded and founded upon the Bible. It is some other hope which in the end turns out to be a frail reed. Only the Bible never fails, but always **upholds** those who trust it.

**117 Hold me up and I will be safe,
And will always look to Your statutes.**

The Septuagint (the Greek translation of the Hebrew Old Testament which is frequently quoted in the New Testament) has "Aid me." In other words, the writer is asking for assistance, help, so that he will be safe from danger in order to be able to give attention to God's **statutes**. If God doesn't do this, he will no longer be around to do so. That is the idea.

There is no bargain here ("God, do this and in exchange I will do that"). No. He wants to go on honoring God before others. But if he doesn't receive help, he will not be able to continue to do so. His desire is to live a life that is pleasing to God and a witness to others. Counselees must be moved from a *quid pro quo* attitude to this one.

**118 You have trampled all who stray from Your statutes
Since their deceit is falsehood.**

The word **trampled** must be understood in the sense of "disdained; made light of." To trample under foot is to show how one detests that which he tramples. God despises all those who stray far from His requirements in

Psalm 119:119

life. They have deceived themselves in thinking they are all right when they are not. They also deceive others. They use false ways in order to deceive. How often a counselee is in trouble because of such **deceit**. Yet he may remember this verse and realize that all the ways of such persons are **trampled** (disdained) by God. That means that he is not alone in doing so. God is not deceived, even though counselees may be. Since God is so concerned about such matters, the counselee may not get overly worked up; he can wait for God to deal with such persons. The next verse deals with that matter. However, he must not fall for false, deceptive ways. The Scriptures will enable him to evaluate and judge such matters correctly.

119 You put away all the wicked of the earth like dross;
  Therefore, I love Your testimonies.

The Psalmist **loves** God's **testimonies** because they condemn sin and reveal the final disposition of sinners and all their works. God will purify His earth as one purifies metals by means of fire that separates the worthless **dross** from the valuable silver. The dross is of no value; it is cast aside. The day of judgment will come in which God will distinguish between those who are His, whose works will stand, and those who are not, whose works will perish with them. The writer loves the Bible because it makes all these things clear. In society in general, one would not be able to ascertain this because he cannot take the long view. The Bible, nevertheless, looks at men and things and their works from the perspective of eternity—which makes all the difference. Counselees who doubt God's control over their affairs must be given the long-term biblical view of life.

**120 My flesh trembles for fear of You,
And I am afraid of Your judgments.**

It is a fearful thing to fall into the hands of the living God. The judgments of God (His Word), in verses like the one quoted in the last sentence, tell of the terror of coming into the presence of the living God as an unforgiven sinner. While no true Christian need fear eternal damnation, the mere fact of hell, nevertheless, should create a certain fear in his heart when he thinks about it. When he reads about God's powerful acts in the Bible, he shudders, shivers, trembles for fear. A counselee who acts too familiarly with God ought to be brought up short and made to think about such matters. Perhaps, then, he would not be so hard on unsaved sinners who are headed in that direction, would pray for their salvation and would witness to them rather than complaining. The Bible certainly speaks of God as a God of love, mercy, grace and compassion. But how fearful it is for those who reject these mercies!

AYIN

**121 What I have done is just and right;
Don't leave me to my oppressors.**

The prayer is that the Psalmist not be **left** in the hands of his persecutors. His plea is based on the fact that he has done what is **right** and **just** toward others. That is, he has acted biblically in relation to them. He has treated his enemies fairly. But they have not responded in kind. He brings in the Scriptures because he has acted in ways that accord with the standards set forth there. His definitions of justice and righteousness are biblical ones. When many people (some counselees) talk about such things, they too

Psalm 119:122

maintain they have been fair to others. But when you press them, what they have done fails to measure up to the biblical standards of justice and righteousness.

Always check out what a counselee means when he says such things. Be sure, like the writer of this verse, he uses the Bible for the standard of what is right and fair. Most people have wrong, self-centered ideas of what is justice for themselves and what is justice for others. So, if you are thinking in biblical categories and he is not, you will be shooting past each other.

**122 Be surety for Your servant;
Don't let proud persons oppress me.**

The Psalmist says, literally, "mix, mingle with me" (in the sense of standing with him, backing him up). In this verse the Bible is said not to be mentioned. Probably there was a scribal error in transmission, though we cannot know this. At any rate, the prayer is for backing. He wants God to stand with him when he faces his enemies. He wants to be able to know that he is not alone. He wants God's help. Plainly, it would seem, he is asking God to do what He has already promised to do in the Bible. If the verse were intact, something along that order probably would have been included. Anyone who loves the Bible as he did and who seeks to follow it as he did would ask only for that which the Bible promises. In the New Testament, Jesus, for instance, promises, "I will not leave you orphans" (John 14:18). He is the one Who will stand behind us in the hour of trial (as a **surety** stands behind another who cannot pay his debts).

**123 My eyes fail for Your salvation
And for Your righteous Word.**

That is to say, his **eyes** were growing blurred, sore of

looking for the fulfillment of God's **righteous Word**, namely, the **salvation** that He promised in the Bible. Here, of course, this is physical **salvation**. The writer had already been saved spiritually. He had waited so long looking that his **eyes** were beginning to play tricks on him. He would think that he saw relief on the horizon, only to discover that he was wrong. His eyes began to fail him (i.e., to give him an inaccurate view of things. Cf. v. 82).

God's help comes only according to His timetable. He does not always intervene when we ask. He has His purpose in delaying. The story of Jesus delaying His response to the word that came from Mary and Martha about Lazarus dying is an example. He actually delayed His coming so that Lazarus would die prior to His arrival. The sisters couldn't understand this. Doubtless, their eyes began to fail as they looked and looked for Him. Yet, as the record shows, Jesus delayed in order to bring them (and all of us) a greater blessing: He would raise Lazarus from the dead.

When we want God to act according to His **righteous Word**, we must take all of it into consideration, including those portions that seem more difficult to bear. The Jews of the first century wanted the crown but refused to accept the cross. For that reason, many of them rejected Christ as Savior. They wanted a victorious Messiah, not a suffering One. But God had other plans. We must always bend our wills to His.

**124 Deal with Your servant according to Your lovingkindness,
And teach me Your statutes.**

The two clauses in the verse fit like hand in glove. The great grace that God communicates to His **servants**

Psalm 119:125

comes through the **teaching of His statutes**. God rarely works apart from His Word. We see in this verse how the Psalmist recognizes the central place that the Scriptures play in communicating grace. Make this clear to your counselees. If they want to experience the **lovingkindness** of God, let them learn from the Bible what it is and how to enter into it. Let them also pray, **teach me Your statutes**.

In the Bible, one learns about God's many acts of lovingkindness. If he fails to know, he will fail to appropriate. How can one be saved unless he hears? He can't (Romans 10). Well, ask this as well: "How can a believer be blessed unless he reads?" Any Christian who neglects the Bible, neglects his own soul. He fails to understand all the wondrous blessings that can be his. How, then, can he even know what to ask for?

Prayer should be intelligent. To pray intelligently is to pray specifically. To pray specifically is to know what to pray for. To know what to pray for is to know God's will. To know what is God's will is to know your Bible. Then, to pray intelligently is to ask God to **deal** with you in accordance with those things that have been learned. Inform counselees of this.

**125 I am Your servant;
Give me discernment that I may know Your testimonies.**

Here, he asks all that we have mentioned in the verse before. But there is one additional factor in view here. He asks for a specific kind of knowledge of God's testimonies: **discernment**. The word means "to separate things out from one another, to divide; to distinguish the things that differ." The modern church lacks discernment. If it is "religious," many will go for it—no matter what is taught.

Psalm 119:126

Some counselees wind up in counseling for that reason. Today the offerings are manifold. One must have at least a modicum of discernment in order to wend his way through them. Many voices are calling him. It is important, therefore, to create a desire in your counselees to learn to discern—how to separate truth from error. Apart from such **discernment**, they will continue to be trapped in all sorts of error and end up in counseling again—or in something worse.

It is the knowledge of God's **testimonies** that gives **discernment** (cf. Hebrews 5).

126 It is time for Yahweh to work;
They have broken Your law.

Ever felt that way? Sure you have. When the newspaper, for instance, headlines the latest act of travesty. When a judge grants custody of a small child to a homosexual father. When a sleazy act of a politician is passed over, and on the same page a Christian is called a radical for his beliefs. You have said, **It is time for Yahweh to work.** "It's time God did something about this!" Yes, men **break** God's **law** and we expect Him to send lightning from the sky to strike them down. Sometimes He does, but not very often. God is a God of mercy, Who is longsuffering. He does not immediately deal with those who oppose His Word. He allows the wicked to run the full length of their chain before He yanks it.

"But," a counselee objects, "how can God let these things continue?" Well, He can precisely because He is God. He does what He wills, and He does it according to His timing. Time that may be long to us is but a blip to God. A thousand years is as a day. Your life and that of your counselee is very short, so you want God to **work** *now*.

Psalm 119:127

God will **work** His work of retribution and judgment—in His day. It is now man's day. And you must teach counselees the virtues of patience and endurance.

**127 Therefore, I love Your commandments
More than gold, even fine gold.**

The more others break God's law, the more the Psalmist **loves** it. As he views the sad state of things, the miserable messes that people get themselves into, he appreciates what he has all the more. The Bible becomes all the more valuable to him. So few possess this treasure that God has so graciously given to him that he will cling to and devote himself to it and the God of Whom it speaks. When he sees divorce, adultery, drug abuse, child pornography, and all the rest, the Bible, in which is found the solution to all of these miseries and which sets forth a very different sort of life of peace and joy, becomes precious in his sight. In comparing it with **gold**—even much of the **finest of gold**—he views it as something that is infinitely more valuable.

**128 Therefore, I count all Your precepts entirely
correct;
I have hated every false way.**

"When I see the mess that others have made of the world and of their lives, even those things in the Bible that I might have doubted I now see to be **entirely correct**. I shall doubt no more, but affirm loudly the **entire** inerrancy of God's Book." That should be the response of every counselee when he sees how seriously he has messed up his own life by failing to follow the Bible. If he does not respond that way, you, as a counselor, have a job to do to help him come to this position. Otherwise, he is going to have a hard time agreeing and complying with

God's holy Word. He must come to it with the attitude that it is more valuable than gold; especially if he has rejected something more valuable than **fine gold** while grasping for wood, hay and stubble. Then, and then only, will he come to the Bible hungering and thirsting for truth to live by. Then only will he be able to say **I hate every false way**.

If he does not **hate** those **false ways** that have led him into trouble then he will not be interested in the Bible. If he is not interested in the Bible, check him out and you may find that this is because he is still in **love** with some **false way**.

It is important, then, to evaluate the counselee's attitude toward the Bible. What value he places on the words of God will have much to do with the progress of counseling. When one comes to **count all God's commandments correct**, as a consequence he will **hate every false way** (especially in himself) because it is in competition with God's **correct** ones. And the **false way** is leading men astray and causing even Christians to dishonor God. Sometimes people wonder why we expose and warn against falsehood in the church. Isn't that unkind? No, just the opposite. The kindest thing one can do is to lead people away from those ways that destroy and dishonor God. It isn't a pleasant task, and it is something for which one is often taken to task, but it must be done. Counselor—here is a mighty verse for *you*.

PE

129 Your testimonies are extraordinary;
Therefore my soul keeps them.

The word translated **extraordinary** is a large one. It

Psalm 119:129

refers to "something so different from other things that it causes wonder." It can even be translated "miraculous." It is the word used to describe Jesus in Isaiah 9:6.

Because the writer has determined that God's **testimonies** are unique (another possible translation) he is devoted to observing them. Of course, that is what it all boils down to, isn't it? If you have a counselee who truly believes that in his hands he holds the very words of the Creator and Ruler of the universe, he should desire with all that is in him to understand and obey them. When a Christian turns elsewhere for help to find direction, it must always be that he has some doubt about God's Word. Indeed, if he persists after adequate explanation that he is rejecting the Word of *God*, there may be reason to question his profession of faith. One believes in Christ as Savior because the unique message of the Bible is that Jesus is that Savior (Romans 10). Why, then, would he want to turn elsewhere for help?

The Bible is unique, **extraordinary**. There is no Book like it. All other books contain error. All other books are written purely by human effort and contain nothing but human thought. The Bible is inerrant. It is the Word of God. Through it the Spirit of God works in order to change and mold the lives of His own. It has all things necessary for life and godliness (It is sufficient). Counselor, when you use the Bible in counseling, it is important that you indicate by that use that you are handling the Word of the living God. You need to communicate the respect, submission and wholehearted belief that this entails. Then, from your handling of the Scriptures, your counselees will gain something of the respect for the Bible that they need.

Psalm 119:130

**130 The unfolding of Your words gives light,
Making naive people discerning.**

The word translated **naive people** is often translated "simple people" both here, and in Proverbs, where it is also used. It has to do with people who are inexperienced, naive in the sense that others may easily "put something over on them." These are vulnerable people (Proverbs 14:15). They don't know much; they are far too trusting of everyone; and they are subject to being led astray. They are fair game for those who would seduce them to believe in some cult or some practices that are way out of line. I am thinking of someone like this when I write. He is "sucked in" to the latest nutritional or herbal craze. He believes in all sorts of conspiracy ideas, and so forth. He fails to examine carefully what others tell him. He is open to everything.

The Christian who is instructed in the Bible, on the other hand, understands that there are many people out there who would "take him" if they could. He will not believe all things. He is Berean-like, searching the Scriptures daily to see if something is or is not true. He has a standard against which he tests everything. He has a fixed point of reference. He is innocent of many things, but he is not naive! He has become a **discerning** person.

In short, he has **light**. That light came to him from the **unfolding** of the Scriptures. The idea in this verse is not that the words of God *enter into* him (though that is true enough), but that the light of the words of God shines forth as they are **unfolded** for him. That is to say, *as he begins to see what they mean*. And this **light** is a **discerning light** (That is the idea in the term sometimes translated understanding). It is a special kind of understanding

109

Psalm 119:131

that enables him to distinguish between the good and the evil, the true and the false.

Some of your counselees have come for help because they have failed to discern error and evil for what it is. They were drawn in by others. There is nothing that they need more than the **unfolding** of the Bible in such a way that its **light** shines on their case. So, you can see the importance of the counselor becoming a careful exegete. The correct interpretation of the Bible is an important part of biblical counseling. You simply cannot do biblical counseling unless you are dedicated to understanding and applying the Bible. One of the main reasons why I have launched on this mammoth undertaking of the interpretation of the New Testament, Proverbs and this book on Psalm 119 with counselors in mind, is because I believe biblical counseling must be just that—the **unfolding** of God's words in order to bring **light** into the lives of counselees. (In this regard reread the story of how Jesus unfolded the Scriptures on the road to Emmaus, and how this made hearts burn within, Luke 24.)

**131 I opened my mouth and panted
Since I longed for Your commandments.**

Like an animal that has been running hard, and now resting **pants** for water, the Psalmist pants for God's Word. The idea behind this figure of speech and in the word **longed** is that of earnest desire to have something. There are times when a counselee enters counseling with just such a desire. He is thirsting for God's answer. He may not know what it is that God wants him to do in this situation but he knows that whatever it is it will be the answer to his problem. He is, as we say, "dying to know God's will."

Psalm 119:132

What a joy it is to counsel such persons! They have come with eyes and ears wide open to Scripture. You'd better give them just that! None of this taking weeks to build a relationship! None of this trying to ascertain all sorts of unnecessary things about them and their situation. A rapid, but thorough history of the problem having been taken and analyzed in the light of Scriptural terminology according to biblical categories, and you turn to the Bible for help. That is what he needs. I am not talking about a hurried-up job, but I am talking about giving the water of life to a thirsty soul. I am talking about stripping off all unnecessary accouterments to counseling that you may have built up. Of course, here again, you must be a biblical exegete, well-versed in the Bible, able to locate and interpret Scripture with alacrity.

**132 Turn to me and favor me
In the manner in which You do to those who love Your Name.**

Here, the **Name** of God seems to stand for all that the Bible says about Him. He is asking that he may find himself in the line of those who have experienced God's blessings down through the years. He believes that he, too, is one of God's children, one who loves the God named and revealed in the Bible, and asks, therefore, that he be treated as God has treated such persons in the past. Of course, he knows all about this treatment from the Bible which sets forth the ways of God with men.

A counselee can ask for nothing more. Presupposing he **loves** God, understands what God is like (knows that His **Names** set forth His character), and is truly in the line of the spiritual descendants of the woman rather than the serpent (Genesis 3:15), he too may seek similar treatment from God. But he must remember that God has many

Psalm 119:133

ways of dealing with His own in His faithfulness (cf. Hebrews 11).

**133 Fix my footsteps in Your Word
And don't allow any evil to rule over me.**

The Psalmist wants to be steady and established in doing God's will as it is expressed in His **Word**. The preposition may be translated **in** or "by." Both are true. To become established, **fixed** *in* biblical ways, one must have his life structured *by* the parameters set forth in the Scriptures. The word **footsteps** indicates his concern to *walk* (live) according to biblical directives.

Here is an ideal for which every counselee should strive, while asking that God will enable him to achieve it. One of the problems counselees have is this: they are unsteady, unpredictable. They vacillate from one way of life to another. They need to become **fixed** in their ways.

It is through the Bible that such establishment may be achieved—and in no other way. It is through the Bible that one learns what God wants him to do, and it is through the Bible that he learns how to do it. Part of that "how-to" is the matter of regular practice, He must learn to put on habitually the new ways of God.

In relationship to this matter of **evil** not **ruling** over him, the discussion in Romans 6-8, could be said to be an exposition of the latter part of this verse. I have dealt with this whole issue in depth in a book entitled, *Winning the War Within.* Since that already exists and is available, I shall say no more about it here.

**134 Redeem me from man's oppression
And I will keep Your commandments.**

The Psalmist wants to be unhindered by the **oppression** that comes from others who do not love God. So he prays that it may be removed. He wants deliverance from some present difficulty that they have caused which stands in the way of doing all he would like to do to honor God. Your counselee may be facing similar hindrances.

The answer, of course, is to direct him also to pray that God will remove from him every obstacle to doing His will. However, until the answer comes, it is incumbent upon him to do all that he *is* able to do. He may not plead that there is nothing that he can do to keep God's precepts until such a time as God answers his prayer. There is always a response to every situation that is appropriate and pleasing to God. It, of course, will be a biblical response. What the Psalmist is praying for is a freer course to do more things for God than he can at the moment. He wants to be **redeemed** (delivered) from the **oppression** that makes it difficult to do as much as he would desire. War sometimes causes such a situation. Lawsuits can do so also. Problems at work can grow to such magnitude that one is stymied. All of these things can be caused by or closely related to the actions of evil persons. The devil is active among his own, inciting them to throw obstacles in the way of God's children. But the Son of God has overcome him; he is no match for Him. Here is one of the ways that you may encourage counselees to deal with his machinations.

**135 Make Your face to shine on Your servant
And teach me Your statutes.**

When God's **face** is said to **shine** on someone, it is the same as if one were saying God approves and is showing His favor to that person. While basking in God's approval, note, the Psalmist does not rest on his laurels. Rather, he takes advantage of the fact to seek to learn more of God's **statutes**. There is no better way or better

Psalm 119:136

time in which to learn of the truths that God has revealed in His Word than when one stands in His favor. He may study lighthearted and guilt-free.

We may also learn in need and trial, it is true. And many counselees do so. But, having emerged from the trial successfully, having satisfied God by one's actions, it is time to study the Bible with added enthusiasm. The trouble is that then is the time when so many settle back, take a rest and become vulnerable to some new problem.

Warn counselees of this tendency. Urge them to continue their Bible study, no longer out of necessity to solve specific problems, but in order to honor God and to walk in His ways in the future. You will be doing counselees a great favor if you point out the problem and warn them against this all-too-frequent tendency of even redeemed sinners.

**136 Rivers of water flow from my eyes
Because they do not keep Your law.**

He speaks here not merely of the effects of evil on himself and on the society around him. There is much to cry about when one looks at that. But, primarily, he is concerned about God—the way in which those who rebel against His law dishonor Him. Whether or not he refers here to unbelievers or to the people of God who are drifting from Him is uncertain. But on both scores the fact of people departing from scriptural ways should bring grief and sorrow to a true lover of God and His Word.

Perhaps it is when those who claim to know and serve Him do so that the deepest grief overcomes one. After all, as sad as it may be, we must expect unsaved persons to fail to **keep**—or want to **keep**—God's **law**. But we expect believers at the very least to desire to know and **keep** it. Yet there is so much lethargy among them. There is so little serious study done. In the area of counseling, so many other ideas, conflicting with those found in the Bible, are proposed in the place of Scripture. These facts are saddening. Counselor, do you grieve over this matter? Is there genuine concern on your part? Have you ever shed a tear over what you see out there? Think about it—and act. "Act?" you say, "How?" In whatever proper ways you can to alter the situation in the church. Speak about it, write about it, vote in meetings the right way, counsel as God wants you. Don't just feel bad; act as you are able. Let your grief not deter you; let it activate you!

TSADHE

**137 You are righteous Yahweh,
And Your judgments are right.**

God's teachings are like His character. The Bible reflects His **righteousness**. It is always **right**—as He is. It is correct, fair, righteous altogether. That is the stance that every counselor must take in the face of opposition from counselees or from others who are trying to influence them not to do what God requires. If the Bible says that a wife must return to her husband (whom she has left for unbiblical reasons), but her parents or friends tempt her to do otherwise, it is necessary for the counselor to affirm that God's Word is **right** about this matter—because He is **righteous**. He does not give unrighteous or incorrect commands. So one must not hesitate to obey, even when he would rather do something else. He must take his stand and not allow others to budge him. It may be necessary to use this verse to convince him of that.

Psalm 119:138

Now I am not saying that one may not reason about the matter in such a way that he is truly attempting to understand. Indeed, the verse itself is an enthymeme in which the reasoning is hidden, but present: if God is **right**, all He does is **righteous**, including all He says in the Bible.

But if the Bible does not allow for reasoning in a given instance, and simply says in unmistakable language that such and such is what God says to do, there is neither need to explain why nor to give a long argument about it. The counselor says, "This is what God's Word requires. You understand that. He expects you to do it. He will bless you when you do, because He is **right**."

**138 Your testimonies that You have commanded
are righteous
And absolutely faithful.**

In the previous verse we considered the righteousness of God's testimonies. They could not be otherwise since God, Who gave them, is righteous. They reflect His nature and His holy will. The same thing is true of His **faithfulness**. His **testimonies** are faithful because God is (cf. I Corinthians 10:13 where Paul insists "God is faithful"). If He is, how can any Christian say that His *Word* is less so? No; and in order to emphasize the fact, the writer declares that His testimonies are **absolutely** (literally, "greatly") **faithful**.

How important for a counselor to know this truth! How reassuring this can be to a counselee who is fearful to take an action that God requires. A counselor may say with total confidence that "If you do what God requires, you can depend **absolutely** on God fulfilling His part. His word is faithful because He is." No one but the biblical

Psalm 119:139

counselor can counsel with such boldness, certainty and confidence—not to speak of authority.

It is a wonder, then, that so many counselors are so apologetic about their advice, even though it is biblical. Why are they hesitant and fearful to proceed as the Bible says? Can it be that they are not truly assured of the **righteousness** and the dependability of God's **testimonies**? If not, then what? If so, then are they also unsure of God Himself? Think about this and about your counseling practice.

**139 My zeal has eaten me up
Because my enemies have forgotten Your
   words.**

This is strong language—a fact that the counselor should not miss. Remember how similar words were used to describe Christ's cleansing of the temple? How **zeal** for His Father's house had **eaten *Him* up**? It means that such righteous anger has consumed him. In both cases, the anger is out of **zeal** for God. It is a **zeal** for God's **words** because they express His will. What is at stake is God's honor. What has enraged him is the way that **enemies** of his have **forgotten** those **words** in their dealings with him.

Do you ever become angry that way? For that reason? Not, mind you, over enemies attacking you, but over their total disregard for God and His Word. There is a great difference between these two things (True discernment distinguishes them). It is not wrong to show anger from time to time in a counseling session when it is aroused in this entirely biblical manner and manifested in a way that allows your counselee to see your concern for God's Word.

Psalm 119:140

**140 Your Word has been tested and found to be very pure;
Therefore, Your servant loves it.**

Like precious metals tried in the fires, the Word of God has always emerged **pure**, free from imperfections, errors, bad advice. There is no dross in it. Over the centuries every possible sort of attack has been leveled against it. Yet, it has come through them all unscathed. The testings of the fires of adversity have served only to reveal its extraordinary **purity**. It is inerrant. It is pure truth, pure love, pure wisdom. Who could want more as a foundation for all his counseling?

No wonder the Psalmist exclaims **Your servant loves it**! Well he might. But the question is—do you? If you don't, why not spend some time thinking, investigating the utter purity of the Bible? Your counselees need to have a counselor who comes into the counseling room with such convictions, loves, and hatreds as the Psalmist exhibits. If you fail to recognize the counseling treasure that God has placed at your disposal, you need to take the time that this Psalmist did to reflect on the purity of God's truth in His Word. Otherwise, your counselees will suffer.

**141 I am small and despised
But I do not forget Your precepts.**

One does not have to be important in the eyes of others to counsel effectively. Here is one who considers himself insignificant (**small**), even **despised**. Don't let that fact turn you off. If you love God and His Word, know the truth of the latter and stand for its purity, you can help many regardless of what others may say and do. You don't need the world's applause. You don't need to be certified by those who **despise** the Bible.

Many counselors have compromised with the world in order to obtain accolades from those who do not take their stand on the Bible. To take that stand in most academic circles (even some that purport to be Christian) is, by definition, to be **despised**. Don't worry if the world (or worldly Christians) look down on you because you want to be biblical. Go ahead and serve God faithfully anyway. His seal of approval is the only one that counts.

The counselor who is willing to be **small** in the eyes of men, if God so wishes, will be large in the eyes of God. That is what is important. And counselees will recognize the fact. That means more to them than a piece of paper on the wall.

Christian counseling is not anti-intellectual. Actually, those who care less for the truth than for men's approval are the ones who are anti-intellectual. You will discover that there is more than enough of this sort of thing that goes on in academic circles. Even in "Christian" academia.

You may be strongly criticized by your "friends" because their actions make them more acceptable in the eyes of the "scholars," while you don't give a fig for that sort of thing. Your approach contrasts with and exposes theirs for what it is. We have all experienced this. You are not alone. Don't let this criticism trouble you for a moment. Just go on doing what you know is right before God and let the chips fall where they may!

**142 Your righteousness is an everlasting righteousness
And Your law is truth.**

Not simply "contains truth;" it is **truth** itself! You counsel on the basis of pure, undefiled truth from God. Why mix in the errors of men?

Psalm 119:143

When the errors and faulty systems of those who refuse to follow God's Word have all passed from the scene—as they always do—God's Word will still be there in all of its beauty and **truth**. Man can produce nothing eternal; only God can do that. The **righteousness** of God, of which the Bible speaks and which it inculcates in His children, is what continues into eternity when all else is left behind. In that day, what others thought will mean very little; what God said will mean everything. Why wait till then? Why not plug into the Source of eternal **truth** now? Why should you be on the wrong side, simply because others are? Whose approval means the most—Man's or God's?

The same appeal may be made to counselees who are inclined to view the opinions of men of too great importance. This attitude should be contrasted with that of the Psalmist in this verse and in the previous one. There is a certain approach to life set forth in this Psalm as a whole. It is a life joyfully and peacefully lived under God's **law**. It is *biblical* living. That is precisely what every counselee needs more than anything else. He must learn to glorify God and enjoy Him forever. How he may do so is found exclusively in the Bible. Make that point over and over again in a variety of ways in counseling.

**143 Affliction and pressure have seized me,
But Your commandments are my delight.**

What else could **delight** in times like that? Surely, it is wonderful to have the Scriptures to turn to when life's **pressures afflict**. There is the place in which he can find direction and guidance. Why, then, doesn't every believer do so? Well, whatever reasons may be adduced, it is clear that they don't. That is why you, counselor, must help him do it. Counseling, in brief, is a matter of helping counselees learn God's ways from the Bible and how to live according to them.

And it is a pleasure to be able to lead counselees, who have been deep in sin or trouble, to that which meets their every need. You are privileged to be engaged in the task. Never forget that. To bring a counselee into an understanding of God's Word, so that he is helped, is a **delight**. It is to honor God before him and to help one more person walk in His way. **Delight** in the work of biblical counseling, believer, and never forget that it was the Scriptures themselves that pointed you in that direction. Others have little delight in counseling because they have such a meager goal—helping people, rather than honoring God! And, their "help" so often is anything but help in the long run (if not sooner).

**144 The righteousness of Your testimonies is everlasting;
Give me discernment and I will live.**

Once more the Psalmist finds himself in a place of danger—with pressures and afflictions such as he mentioned in verse 143 close at hand. He is near death. But by following God's **righteous** ways, which are not temporary and changeable, but permanent and dependable in every age because they are **everlasting**, he knows he can find the right way through the trouble and **live**.

If a person can turn to God's Word in time of near death, surely your counselee can find help in his affliction, which probably doesn't even approach that by way of severity. Show him how the Psalmist stakes his very life on the Bible. Ask, "Can't you, then, depend on God's Word for something else?"

Psalm 119:145

KOPH

145 I cried with my whole heart; answer me Yahweh.
I will keep Your statutes.

One of the conditions for offering acceptable prayer is fervency (cf. James 5:16). Here, as well as in many of the verses in this section, the Psalmist speaks fervently out of distress. The problem of waiting for God to respond to prayer that is made from the **heart** often looms large in counseling. The first consideration is that no one can keep God's **statutes** without the power of the Holy Spirit. Prayer is an essential factor, therefore, in doing so. It is right for counselees to pray.

Counselees become troubled over not receiving **answers** when they too have cried out from the bottom of their **hearts**. But, as we have already noted, God answers in His way and in His time—which is always the very best **answer** for His children. They need to learn that this is so. The essential element here is to exercise faith in waiting.

146 I cried to You; save me
And I will keep Your testimonies.

There is nothing new in this verse. See, therefore, previous verses dealing with the same theme.

147 I went before the dawning of the morning and cried out;
I hoped in Your Word.

To get up early in the **morning** (as when Abraham got up early to sacrifice his son) means that one puts what he is doing in a place of priority. It is no after thought.

Psalm 119:148

Nor is there any reluctance about it. Here, wherever it was that he was going to pray, he got up and **went** while it was still dark.

Expecting God to keep His **Words**, he called out for the help He was promised in the Bible. The fact that prayer is made for that which has already been promised emphasizes a point that often needs to be made in counseling. That is, it is necessary to follow the means that the Bible sets forth in order to receive the results that it promises. Too often the latter are emphasized without concern for the former. Here, the Psalmist is so oriented toward the means (prayer) that he puts it first on his agenda. Counselees must not be allowed to complain about God not keeping His promises when they fail to observe the biblical means by which these promises come about. If prayer is no priority to them why should they complain if God doesn't answer when they wish Him to do so? And the conditions for the answer to promises must also be recognized: God promises to answer prayer in His way, in His time.

**148 My eyes go before the night watches
That I might meditate on Your Word.**

That is, prior to each **watch** during the **night** (There were three; cf. Judges 7:19), he opened his eyes in order to **meditate** on the Scriptures. Often, in the stillness of the night one can concentrate better than during the day with the noise and interruptions that occur. Moreover, it seems that the writer could not wait until the next morning to find out something that he needed to know from God's **Word**.

"When," you might ask a counselee who maintains that he has searched the Scriptures to no avail, "have you gotten up in the middle of the night to do so because it

Psalm 119:149

was of such great importance to you?" If one is concerned enough to find out God's will, he will do everything possible to discover it—which, at times, may mean even missing sleep. Earnestness is clearly in evidence in this verse.

149 Hear my voice according to Your lovingkindness, Yahweh; According to Your judgments give me life.

Here, as in many of the other verses in this Psalm, the writer appeals to the **lovingkindness** of God as it is set forth in the Bible. He asks for **life** in a time of danger and asks for the salvation that is promised to God's children in the Bible.

150 Those who pursue wickedness draw near; They are far from Your law.

What a picture of some people! They **draw near** to **pursue wickedness** and distance themselves from God's **law**. That is how it is. One cannot move in both directions at once; they are opposite one another. He either goes one way or the other. Counselees must be shown the utter antithesis between God's **law** (in which is found nothing but goodness) and **wickedness**. The two cannot be mixed as many try to do. Instead, intentionally or not, they end up **pursuing wickedness**.

The Psalmist sees them headed his direction: **they draw near**. He is alarmed at what they will do next, so he turns to God, asking Him to do something about it. After all, they are ignoring His **law**. That means they are opposing Him. If they are opposing God, he may expect God to deal with them about their sin. This, like the rest of the verses in this section, is a cry for help—though implied rather than stated.

**151 You are near, Yahweh,
And all Your commandments are truth.**

There is an interplay between the words **draw near, far from** (v. 150) and **near** in this verse. Let those who pursue wickedness (and presumably will attempt to do so when they arrive at the place where I am) do so. What does it matter when God is **near**? In other words, they will have to deal not only with me, but ultimately, with God Himself. They think they are coming to oppress me, but actually, they are coming to fight with God. That is hardly a fair fight; there is no way in which they can win.

That is an important insight for counselees to recognize. Every time wicked persons approach a believer, in whom the Holy Spirit dwells, to **pursue** their **wicked** ways, they are also approaching God in him. The conflict that ensues will be a conflict with Him. That is reassuring. It is amazing to know that God never leaves us alone; that (as Christ promised) He will be with us "always" in the Person of His Spirit. Others are coming **near** to harm; God is **near** to help.

That they will have to deal with Him is what the Bible teaches. It is on the basis of the biblical data that the writer can affirm that God is **near**. He knows that it is true since he is certain that **all** of His commandments are true. That is the foundation for all of the hopes of the believer. I have already said much about this in the exposition of other verses.

**152 Of old I have known from Your testimonies
That You have founded them forever.**

Is this circular reasoning? Yes. All reasoning, at bottom, is circular. One starts with his presuppositions and goes from there. The writer knows from the Bible about

Psalm 119:153

the Bible. But because he also knows the Author of the Book, there is no problem accepting anything that the Bible says about itself as true since He knows that the divine Author is truth itself. From the beginning of his salvation the Psalmist has known that Bible truth is unshakable. It is a fundamental thought in this entire Psalm that one can depend on God's Word because it will not change. When God says something, you can count on it. The utter dependency of the Psalmist on God's words is the underlying theme of all that he writes. Counselees also must trust the trustworthy Word.

RESH

**153 Look at my affliction and deliver me
Since I do not forget Your law.**

There is nothing new in this verse. All of the sentiments it expresses have been dealt with earlier. It is easy to **forget** when the pressure is on. The Psalmist is aware of the temptation. It would not be remiss for counselors to send out counselees from counseling with this verse in hand to remind them that during the next trial they should remember God's **law**. That is to say, turn to it for the comfort, the encouragement and the direction that is needed. Rather than **forget** during a time of **affliction**, that is precisely when it is necessary to remember and use the Bible.

Remember, too, the Bible sets forth a variety of ways in which God **delivers**. It is not always (nor usually?) the way we might think or desire. But He knows best and we can trust Him to do the right thing.

Psalm 119:155

**154 Plead my cause and redeem me;
According to Your Word give me life.**

Here, the new element is the Psalmist calling upon God to become his Advocate, One Who will **plead** his **cause** before the court and **redeem** him from a severe sentence. When no one else will, God takes up the cause of His own. He also becomes the advocate for widows and orphans and those who are vulnerable and helpless. When God goes to court, there is no one who can stand against Him. Even Satan, the great adversary, the accuser of the brethren, wilts in front of the evidence of Christ's satisfaction which answers all charges against the believer.

Whatever the charge was (which doubtless was a false charge leveled against him by his enemies) it would seem that his life was in jeopardy because of it. Of course, it may be that the forensic language is but a figurative way of framing his prayer. Either way, it is important to inform counselees that it is proper for them to pray this way. Often they *are* truly involved in legal matters of one sort of another. This prayer, in such situations, is most appropriate—and should be encouraging.

**155 Salvation is far from the wicked
Since they do not seek Your statutes.**

This is as clear a statement as one could want about the exclusiveness of Christianity. Those who turn down the message of the Bible which speaks about the death and resurrection of Jesus Christ, will be lost eternally. There is salvation in no other (Acts 4:12). And the message that tells about Him is found in the Bible alone. Unless one believes the Bible message (which, of course may be mediated by tract, book, word of mouth, etc., but stems ultimately from the Bible) he cannot be saved. **Salvation is far from** him.

Counselees, being Christians, need to hear this fact if they do not already know it. Their friends and loved ones who are without Christ are also without **salvation**. That means they have a responsibility to tell them about the Savior. Part of the counselor's responsibility is to emphasize this fact whenever it is appropriate to do so. Many times, solving problems in counseling provides the very opening for a witness to the Gospel that is needed.

**156 Your tender mercies are large, Yahweh;
According to Your judgments give me life.**

How does the Psalmist know that God's **tender mercies** are great? He has read about them in the Bible, and he has experienced the same in his life. His experience would count for little by itself; all sorts of people claim experiences with God—Mormons, New Agers, etc. But when one reads about those mercies that God has (or will) show His people in the Bible, and then avails himself of them, his experience corresponds to the inerrant Word. That is different. Experience, to be valid, must be instigated and interpreted by the teachings of the Bible. Counselees must never interpret the Bible by their experience, but the other way around: experience must be interpreted by the Bible.

Once again, in his extremity, the Psalmist calls out for **life**.

**157 My persecutors and my enemies are many
[But] I do not turn aside from Your
testimonies.**

There is no doubt that one of the things that his **enemy** wants is for your counselee to **turn aside** from his

Psalm 119:158

commitment to walk the Christian life. And, under pressure, many do. Today, in our soft culture, it doesn't even take serious persecution to effect this sad result. All it takes is ostracism, scorn and the like. Indeed, because one doesn't want to be embarrassed, he will soft-pedal his beliefs in the Bible (as a counselor or as a counselee) in order to "stay on the right side of" those who might otherwise ridicule him. How many melt under the slightest provocation! Here is a fundamental problem with which every counselor must deal—in his own life and in that of the counselee. If you are not doing well in this regard, counselor, you'd better get your own life straightened out so that you will be able to speak honestly, when necessary, to counselees about it.

**158 I saw traitors and was grieved
Because they did not keep Your Word.**

Here, doubtless, he speaks of **traitors** against God. Here were those who had professed faith, but later turned to the enemy, denouncing their former profession. They were traitors to the kingdom of God—covenant breakers. That is a desperate condition in which to find oneself (cf. Hebrews 6, 10). The Psalmist was sickened over the fact. There were some in this group, it seems, that he had known personally. And he now saw what had happened to them. Most of all, he was **grieved** about the dishonor they brought upon God. Traitors always dishonor their country and its King.

Because there is a pseudo-gospel preached today in evangelical circles, in which one is asked to "take Jesus into your heart" (an unbiblical expression which says nothing about His sacrificial, substitutionary death for sins and His resurrection from the dead; cf. I Cor. 15), counselor, you will see more and more of this. If one

Psalm 119:159

thinks he was saved when he believed, but actually was not, he may show up in counseling claiming salvation on a wrong basis. Explain the gospel plainly; it may be exactly what he needs to keep him from entirely turning his back on Jesus Christ. Evangelism, when needed, is an essential element; it makes counseling possible. It is precounseling.

159 See how I love Your commandments Yahweh;
According to Your lovingkindness give me life.

This verse reiterates what I have considered before.

160 The sum total of Your Word is true
And every one of Your righteous judgments endures forever.

What a marvelous affirmation of faith in God's Word! From beginning to end—its **sum total**—God's **Word** is **true**. In order that no one might misunderstand, he goes on to explain **every one of Your righteous judgments endures forever**. He is talking about the Bible—every sentence and word of it. It is all **true**. It is lasting. That must be the conviction and the continual affirmation of every biblical counselor. If it is not, his counseling cannot rightly be called biblical. No one has the right to pick and choose what he wants to accept from the Scriptures. It must be taken as a whole or not at all. The Psalmist knew this and said so in so many words. You must take this same position, counselor. And you must not allow counselees to pick and choose from the Bible either.

Psalm 119:162

SHIN

**161 Princes have persecuted me without cause,
But my heart fears Your Word.**

The idea to be gleaned from this verse is that it is your task to help your counselee to stand tall in the face of oppressive authorities (he will not be facing **princes**) without **fear**. Everyone fears something or someone. Here, it is a choice between fearing an earthly power or a heavenly One, as it is manifested in His **Word** (cf. Matthew 10:29; Isaiah 8:12, 13). What the Psalmist fears is that he might violate God's **Word**. When a counselee acquires that sort of fear, he is well on his way toward solving his problem.

The point of the verse, however, is that this persecution is **without cause**. The counselee often finds himself in situations that he didn't bring on himself. Such persecution is especially heinous. But when he knows that what is happening is not his own doing, that he is not the one who provoked the problem, he has no reason to fear anyone but God. When he has the fear of God in his heart, is content to obey His Word and is concerned not to break it, he will not be deterred from keeping His commandments—even though threatened by earthly powers.

**162 I rejoice at Your Word—
As one who has found great spoil.**

The word **spoil** means "that which was gained by plunder." Typically, it would be hidden or buried somewhere. Here, the picture is of one coming upon such a cache, a large and very valuable treasure. Such a find (Captain Kidd's buried treasure, for instance) would make a person very happy. He'd be rich overnight.

Psalm 119:163

But how many think of finding truth in God's **Word** that way? Shouldn't they? Of course—the Psalmist did. In this Book are treasures that are greater than riches untold. They are treasures that cannot be lost, that will not pass to another, that one can carry with him when he dies! Here is a treasure that can improve his relationship with others, make him wise above all his teachers and bring him into favor with God. Why do not counselees see this? Is it that we counselors fail to exhibit the joy of discovery that the Psalmist evidenced when speaking about the Bible? That is worth thinking about. Surely, we want this for our counselees, don't we?

**163 I hate and despise lying,
But I love Your law.**

Now there is an important contrast: **hate/love**; **lying/**God's **law**. And this vivid contrast demands a choice. Will the counselee settle for something less than the absolute truth? Will he settle for lies of men rather than hold out for the truth of God? What does he **love**; what does he **despise**? Often you must put the choices before him in exactly those terms.

A pretty good gauge of one's **love** for the Bible is how much he **hates** opposing falsehood. When it comes to evaluating the theories of men, it is not a mere academic matter, as many would have it. They want to discuss human theories dispassionately and become upset only when others of us do not. *They* **hate** any emotional writing that exposes falsehood for what it is. Evidently, they have read little of the Reformers. For the Psalmist it is a matter of **hating** what dishonors God and His **Word**, and does harm to people. It is sad to see Christians who fail to understand this, and who in the name of tolerance (or sophistication) buy into the academic approach—to

Psalm 119:165

lies! You must care enough about God's truth and the welfare of your counselees that you, too, **hate lying**. There is much that could be said in this regard, but it is important to stand with the Psalmist in this matter. Where do you stand, counselor?

**164 I praise You seven times a day
For Your righteous judgments.**

Do *you*? Does your counselee? If not, why not? What is lacking? Seven is an idiom for "often, repeatedly" (cf. Proverbs 24:16). **Praising** God for the Bible is an activity that is found all too seldom among so-called Bible-believers. It is interesting that many of those who call themselves biblical counselors have nothing but praise for the theories of men who hated God and His Word, but sneer at those who stand with the Bible alone. It is time to see this situation change. Will you become a change-agent in the church of Jesus Christ?

**165 Those who love Your law have great peace,
And they have no occasion for stumbling.**

What a wonderful fact! What a treasure for which to praise God! Here is what counselees lack: **peace**. And here, in one brief summary statement is how to obtain it. Many counselees also have trouble with temptation. The way to meet temptation (as the Lord Jesus demonstrated in dealing with the tempter) is with Bible truth. In other words, precisely what counselees need to resist temptation is what the Bible supplies. There is no need to **stumble** and fall if one is on the biblical path doing what God requires. **Peace** comes from knowledge applied in the assurance that God will accept what he is doing. Obstacles may appear in the counselee's way, but when he knows his Bible, he also knows the way around (or

Psalm 119:166

through) them. Those who **love** God's **law** will know how to resist the devil so that he will flee from them (James 4:7).

**166 Yahweh, I hoped for Your salvation
And have done what You commanded.**

There is no doubt that this is the recipe for joy and peace. Every counselee must be pointed in this direction. The **hope** here is in the expectation (the meaning of the biblical word for **hope**) of God's blessings of protection and guidance. The **salvation** in view is rescue from the plots and the machinations of those who oppose. That which is **commanded** is the requirements of the Bible. No one in trouble can find a better (or equal) solution to his problem.

**167 My soul has kept Your testimonies,
And I greatly love them.**

Once again, **soul** is the poetic way of saying "I" do such and such. He is affirming his basic allegiance to and compliance with God's commandments. But, as he often says, it is not mere servile obedience that is in view; rather, it is **love** for His Word that motivates him to obey. There is a difference between loving the task and loving the Lord Who assigned it. A counselee may not enjoy doing God's will—it could be irksome or dangerous. But he should love the Lord Whose will it is. He **loves** and **keeps** God's **testimonies** because he wants to please Him. And in addition, he knows that, in the long run, doing so will reap eternal blessings.

**168 I have kept Your precepts and testimonies;
Indeed, all my ways are before You.**

The Psalmist appeals to God to verify his claim. It is **before** Him Who knows everything that we do and say that he makes the claim. When a counselee can repeat these words with sincerity he too will know God's blessings on his life here, and hereafter.

When dealing with counselees it is appropriate to ask, when they claim that they are **keeping** God's commandments (but there is no discernible change in their situation), if they can declare that **before** God (i.e., in His presence). Make it clear that they may be able to fool you as a counselor for a while but they can never fool God. And God not only knows the facts, He is ready to respond to any false statements on their part.

Often a husband or a wife will make claims that he or she is doing everything that is required, but the spouse denies it. How can you know who is telling the truth? In time you probably will find out. But at the moment, in such a situation, it might be of importance to read this verse and explain that you may not be aware of who is lying and who is telling the truth, but that really doesn't matter. God knows and you will leave it in His hands to adjudicate the matter.

TAU

**169 Let my cry come near You Yahweh;
Give me discernment by Your Word.**

Again, the Psalmist pleads for **discernment** which he knows comes by God's **Word**. That is the correct approach. The counselee isn't supposed to pray for **dis-**

Psalm 119:170

cernment and wait until it suddenly strikes him out of the blue. No, he is to pray for it to come from his study of God's **Word**. Too many want wisdom, discernment and knowledge handed to them on a silver platter. It doesn't come that way. These things come through the disciplined, regular study and application of the Scriptures to life's circumstances. And usually, that is only "by reason of practice" in interpreting and utilizing biblical teaching (Hebrews 5).

**170 Let my prayer for mercy come before You;
Deliver me according to Your Word.**

The term translated by the words **prayer for mercy** means "to ask for pity, for favor." It is the prayer of one who knows that he deserves nothing from God, but knows from his reading of the Bible how merciful He is to those who call upon Him in supplication. He is once again calling for **deliverance**—the cry of every counselee, no matter what his problem may be.

**171 My lips will utter praise
When You have taught me Your statutes.**

The only perfect teacher is God. The Psalmist wants Him to be his teacher. And he promises to praise God for what He teaches. The Holy Spirit dwells within each true believer to enable him to understand and apply the Bible. that means every Christian has God as his teacher as well. Thus, the counselee should recognize that he also can pray this prayer.

But he must not miss the latter part of it. He too should be ready and anxious to gratefully thank and **praise** God when He does enable him to learn and apply His truth to his life. Every counselor would do well, at the conclusion of each successful counseling case when he is ready to dismiss the counselee, to take time for praise and thanksgiving with him.

172 My tongue will answer Your Word
Because all of Your commandments are righteousness.

When God speaks, obedient Christians listen. When God speaks, they also **answer**. As one reads the Bible he is being addressed by God. That means he is in a conversation with Him. It is not much of a conversation when only one person speaks. So the counselee should be taught to answer God. He should say "Yes" to His commands. He should ask, "How?" when he is perplexed about how to implement a command. He should explain his weaknesses and plead for the strength and help that is needed, and so on. Just as this Psalmist does, only not in an academic fashion; it is to be heard and **answered** in a living conversation with God. God speaks in the Bible; the counselee answers in prayer and obedience.

It is not impossible to teach this dialog to counselees in the counseling room. Find a command of God that is directly applicable to the counselee, read and explain it. Then, having used this verse to motivate him, ask him to tell God in prayer what he is going to do about it. Ask him to tell God anything else that he thinks is important to say. In other words, get him started on the Bible/prayer conversation with God that this verse involves.

173 Let Your hand help me
Since I have chosen Your commandments.

Obviously, in the Bible/prayer interchange between God and the counselee, the words of this verse may be one of his prayers. "I will need help to obey Your **commandments**. I have **chosen** to do so, but it will be hard.

Psalm 119:174

Help me in the ways that You know I shall need such help."

And don't fail to note that obedience is a **choice**. A counselee will not naturally do God's will. He must *determine* to do so. It is a choice in which it is necessary to move out in obedience asking God to **help** as you do. The verse does not recommend sitting around waiting for some sort of strength or wisdom from God before acting. Rather, it envisions a counselee making the right choice and, as he goes forward in obedience, asking for God's personal assistance. The strength often comes in the doing.

**174 Yahweh, I have longed for Your salvation,
And Your law is my delight.**

Again, this is a verse that, in substance, has been dealt with already.

**175 Let my soul live and it will praise You,
And let Your judgments help me.**

Here it is the **judgments** of the Lord that help a counselee to find life. He wants to be delivered from death by the counsel of the Word. Many a counselee has found that it was precisely what the Scriptures did that delivered him. The Scriptures are designed to help people even in the most extreme circumstances. That is one reason why it is ludicrous for pseudo-counselors to say that a person's problem is "too deep" for the pastor. A pastor who knows and can use the Bible effectively wields the greatest power imaginable in helping others.

Don't be intimidated by those who would scorn the biblical counsel that you offer. It is they who are woefully inadequate. Always uphold the power of the Word used by the Spirit in the lives of His own. There is nothing that can begin to approach it.

**176 I have gone astray like a lost sheep;
Seek Your servant since I do not forget Your law.**

The Psalmist recognizes his tendency to **stray** from God's pathway. So he calls on Yahweh, his Shepherd (Psalm 1:1), to **seek** and restore him when he does. He knows that he cannot be sinless; he knows his weaknesses. And he doesn't hesitate to call on God for help. Every counselee, during sessions and at the end of a case, might also pray this prayer. Notice how the Psalmist ends with it? It recognizes both something about himself as a wandering sheep and something about God as a Shepherd. That relationship is a very salutary one (cf. Isaiah 53:5).

CONCLUSION

Psalm 119 is full of help for the counselor and for his counselees. Individual verses have much to say. Many ought to be memorized. Others could be grouped to present all sides of an issue. But if they tell us one thing it is that the true saint of God is one who loves God's Word and does it. His life in prosperity and in trouble is centered in the Scripture's promises and help. The Psalm should make it clear to all who study it how important God considers His Book and how He works through it. The Psalm should give great confidence to the biblical counselor.

Counselees should identify with this Psalm. So much of it deals with afflictions and sufferings of all sorts. Throughout, the Psalmist, while longing to do all that God commands, confesses his failures. It is a counselee's

Psalm 119:176

Psalm. That is why I have presented it to counselors and counselees for their mutual help. Learn all you can about it. Read it through often. Mark various verses that refer to specific problems and make notes in the margin of your Bible to that effect for rapid location. You will want to do this since you will increasingly find yourself referring to this Psalm in counseling.

It is my earnest hope that I have been able to do three things in this book:

1. Stimulate a new interest in the Psalm.
2. Explain some of the verses that may have been obscure.
3. Note some of the ways that these verses will help in biblical counseling.

If I have achieved something of each of these purposes, the time I spent working on the Psalm will have been well-spent. If I achieve none of them, nonetheless, I can testify that working on this Psalm has been a great blessing to me. It has made me appreciate the Bible all over again.